Robert Powell

Lesson Planning:
the menu

RCP Training and Consultancy
MOTIVATE AND ENGAGE LEARNERS

Published by RCP Training and Consultancy
56 Stockton Lane
Stafford
ST17 0JS

First published April 2016
© Robert Powell 2016

ISBN-13: 978 0 9935514 0 6
ISBN-10: 0 9935514 0 6

Editor: Pat Winfield
Designer: Neil Hawkins, ndesign

Printed in Great Britain by Cambrian Printers, Wales

Contents

Profile of Robert Powell

Robert Powell has spent a lifetime in education, as a classroom teacher, Head of Department, Head of Year, Deputy Head and Headteacher. He led Blurton High School (now called Ormiston Sir Stanley Matthews Academy) in Stoke-on-Trent for just over four years during which time the school nearly doubled its higher grade GCSE passes and its SATs scores at Key Stage 3.

Before taking up his headship in 1997 he worked for eight years in publishing and consultancy. He was the co-founder of Network Educational Press and Network Consultancy, but left to set up Robert Powell Training and Publications in 1996. He has written nine books including his two most recent, *Feedback and Marking*, and *Outstanding Teaching, Learning and Assessment: the Handbook*. The highly successful *Raising Achievement* and *Active Whole-Class Teaching* were amongst his earlier publications. He has worked on INSET with over a 2000 primary and secondary schools, was a consultant to the SSAT working with Academies and has led inset with dozens of FE colleges and with most of the highly performing Sixth Form Colleges across the UK. He also worked as a consultant to the DfE some years ago in the Innovation Unit. He is renowned for his challenging and humorous style of presentation.

What customers say about Robert's training sessions

Robert's INSET on Personalised Learning was just the 'shot in the arm' that my staff, ranging from Nursery to Year 6, needed at the start of a busy term

Antony J.W. Hudson, Headmaster, St George's College Junior School

Robert Powell's visionary approach highlights consistency rather than conformity and inspires the hearts and minds of teachers. I can honestly say that his philosophy, and the practical strategies he is renowned for, have had a bigger impact upon my school than any other author or trainer I have met in my 18 years as a headteacher.

Jim Godfrey, Headteacher, Marston Vale Middle School, Beds

Money well spent! Rarely does the booking of an outside speaker lead to educational transformation. However, Robert's ideas have challenged our preconceptions in a hugely positive way.

Neil Finlay, Headteacher, Walton High School, Stafford

It was an excellent day, probably the best we have had in this college.

Mike O'Hare, Principal, Holy Cross Sixth Form College, Bury

Simply, Robert elicited from the Stowe staff the most positive response we've ever had to a communal day's INSET.

Stephen Hirst, Director of Studies, Stowe School

Introduction

The design and role of lesson plans

There is no single format for lesson planning. Some leadership teams in schools and colleges reject form-filling and allow their staff to plan lessons in whatever way they choose. Some adopt a very simple lesson-planning form with just a few key headings that take little time for teachers to complete. Others design a highly complex document with multiple headings and insist that teachers complete it in detail before each lesson. Some schools and colleges change their policies over time. A highly detailed lesson-planning policy may be necessary during a transitional period. For example, a lack of effective planning may have been identified by leadership or inspection teams as one of the causes of low achievement. The introduction of rigorous planning forms and rigid lesson structures may be two of the strategies introduced to remedy the problem.

The leaders of good schools and colleges recognise, however, that such strategies are no more than short term – they may move them out of a 'failing' category, but to persist with the policy may actually prevent them from achieving 'outstanding' status. Indeed, inspectors in schools and colleges in England now look for 'evidence of planning' and do not insist on seeing a detailed lesson plan. Outstanding teachers also need to be released from the straitjacket of the rigid lesson structure and allowed to show their passion. The 3/4/5-part lesson, often based on a 'learning cycle', does not work for all teachers, and inspectors do not expect to see such lessons as the norm. Readers will find, among the techniques and strategies in the 'menu' that follows, ideas that excite them – lessons that will engage, motivate, support and challenge learners.

Many of them will require planning time, and teachers will be unable to find this time if they are required to complete detailed lesson-planning forms. This handbook and the app version will help in this process. The content provides a menu of outstanding techniques that can be turned into a lesson plan in minutes; creative and exciting lessons with rigorous planning.

Add your own techniques

The techniques described on the menu for each section are not meant to be an exhaustive list – there will be many excellent strategies used by teachers that are not included. That is why the app version allows teachers to import their own menus of outstanding techniques. There are no starters or plenaries included in the menus and those teachers who want to use them can simply add their own menu list to the menu in the app. The menus in each chapter of this handbook are simply exemplars of how schools or teams of teachers within a school or across a group of schools can bring together the best strategies and techniques and store them in a coded handbook ready to use in lesson planning.

The menus that are included, however, in this handbook can be used by many to widen their own repertoire of techniques and this process can be used to stimulate discussion within teams about other ideas that can be added. Many teachers are quite conservative in their lesson planning, using tried and trusted methods time and again. There is nothing wrong with this, but if you ask learners, they invariably tell you that the best lessons are those when the teacher does something *different*; learners love variety.

The handbook can be used by all teachers, regardless of the situation in which they work. The concept of the 'menu' is central to this book. Restaurants offer customers menus that range from the simple one-course meal to the seven- or eight-course gourmet experience. Diners make choices both on the number of courses and on the content of each course. This lesson-planning menu does the same. Menus produced collaboratively by teams of teachers would allow teachers to have rich menus to access in the planning process.

A range of 'courses' or lesson ingredients follow, with each course offering a wide range of choices. Most of the key headings used by schools and colleges in lesson planning are included, and this allows users of the handbook to make choices based on the situation in which they work or simply on their professional judgement. Menus produced by teams of teachers might use different key headings – often to match the key headings in lesson-plan templates.

The app version allows teams of teachers to produce their own version of the menus that follow and import them into the app. So, for example, a year or phase team in a primary school or a department in a secondary school or college could collaborate to publish a handbook of outstanding practice containing all the best ideas for each lesson plan heading. This can be then used in the app in the same way as the menus in this handbook are used in the final chapter.

The menus for this handbook now follow and how they, or alternative handbooks produced in-house by schools or colleges, might be used follows in the final chapter.

Classroom Organisation

Alternative headings

Room layout

Seating plans

Use of groups

Introduction

Classroom organisation covers two key areas: the arrangement of tables or desks and seating plans. Experienced teachers will almost certainly have experimented during their careers with different arrangements for their classrooms or teaching spaces. Some of these are set out in the menu below. However, some teachers, for example in practical workshops or science laboratories, may have fixed furniture and so have little choice over the organisation of tables. Other teachers, who do not have the luxury of their own teaching spaces, may have to work with the arrangement they inherit on arrival in the room.

Seating plans are used by many teachers and they too vary depending upon (a) the philosophy of the teacher, (b) the guidance issued by the leadership and (c) the context of the lesson.

Key issues

Classroom organisation can have a major influence on the success or otherwise of teaching, learning and assessment. Teachers need to ask themselves the following questions when deciding upon the arrangement of tables:

- If the lesson plan involves moving from whole-class teaching to small group or independent activity, the arrangement must facilitate this; will the movement of tables in mid-lesson disrupt the learning atmosphere?
- Some teachers adopt active learning approaches involving role-play or regular movement around the room – does the arrangement allow this?
- Teachers may, on occasions, want to hold one-to-one or small group tutorials – where will these tutorials take place?

Seating plans can also make a significant contribution to successful teaching, learning and assessment. They can be used to meet a number of different needs:

- Reducing the chances of poor behaviour by separating known miscreants.
- Organising seating so that learners with different levels of skill, confidence or language can make use of peer support.
- Arranging seating to facilitate focus groups where learners are working on different aspects of a project.
- Seating groups by ability so that either the teacher or LSA can target support more economically and set differentiated tasks.

Teachers may, of course, use all of the above at different times. The menu that follows does not include examples from the early years' classroom. Anyone privileged enough to visit such a classroom will wonder at the inventiveness of the teachers and carers who have created the most amazing environment for small children.

Every space will have been designed to stimulate the senses, and no drawing or sketch can capture the igloos, the washing lines, the cushions, the textures, the sounds and the smells of such classrooms.

A1   Rows of tables or desks, random seating[1]

The tables or desks are arranged in rows with individuals or pairs facing the front. The seating is random.

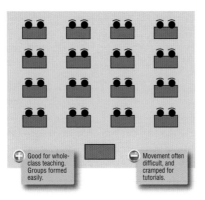

⊕ Good for whole-class teaching. Groups formed easily.

⊖ Movement often difficult, and cramped for tutorials.

A2   Rows of tables or desks, teacher's seating plan

The tables or desks are arranged in rows as in A1 with individuals or pairs facing the front. The seating plan is chosen by the teacher.

A3   Rows of tables or desks, teacher's seating plan for group work

This is the same as A2 with the addition that the seating plan allows groups to form easily by each pair simply turning around to face the pair behind. The teacher has chosen the groups.

This arrangement is ideal for teachers who want to switch from whole-class teaching, where all the learners face the front, to small group activity where they work in groups of four. The teacher has been careful to ensure that when each pair turns around, the resulting group is fit for purpose. The teacher does not want to create conflict with the choice of groupings.

A4 Cabaret with seating plan

In this arrangement, the tables are grouped for four students, facing each other in pairs. None of the learners are seated on the front edge with their backs to the teacher.

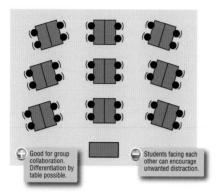

Good for group collaboration. Differentiation by table possible.

Students facing each other can encourage unwanted distraction.

This type of arrangement is very common. Learners are not allowed to sit on the front edges of any of the tables – that would mean they had their backs to the teacher, which is not a good idea in terms of classroom management. The cabaret arrangement provides a number of options in terms of seating plans. The four learners can be grouped for peer support. (See also *Support Groups* in Section F on differentiation.) For example, an EAL student might sit next to someone who speaks their native language and opposite two speakers of English. This combination helps such learners to get support from a friend while also learning spoken English from their group partners opposite.

Similarly, the placing of two confident students together but opposite two weaker learners provides teachers with a range of options:

- Group collaboration involving all four learners
- Peer coaching in pairs across the table
- Peer testing with their partner (see section on Questioning).

During whole-class teaching, learners are required to turn their chairs sideways so that they face the teacher. During group activity they turn back to face their partners opposite.

A5   Roles and responsibilities

Rules and responsibilities in each cabaret group are clearly
defined. Roles such as Chairperson and Scribe are rotated and
responsibilities allocated in group research.

Most teachers who have used group activities will have
experienced at some time the group where one learner does all
the work and the others sit about talking. When the group is
then praised for its efforts, the lone 'worker' feels aggrieved.
The likelihood of this situation arising can be reduced if the
teacher allocates roles. In a brainstorming session, for example,
one learner is the Chairperson whose role is to ensure the group
performs the task and meets its deadline. Another learner is the
Scribe who must record all the ideas of the group. But the rule
that makes this effective is that the Scribe must not only record
the idea but in brackets must record **whose idea** it was.
Everyone will want their name on the list!

Discrimination	Whose idea?
Women's pay in equal jobs	Amanda
% of women in senior management	Karl
Maternity rights	Juan

If the seminar group is asked, for example, to plan a
presentation together, the teacher can make use of a simple
group planning form.

Who	What	When	Teacher

The group has to record what each person is doing in the
presentation and the date when it will be ready. Teachers will
sign off the plan when they are happy with it but may intervene
if, for example, any of the learners are working at too high or too
low a level: *my role is to colour in the front page*…

This type of planning form is very useful post-16 when small groups are required to use private study to plan a talk or presentation for a later lesson. Before they leave the previous lesson, the teacher has a copy of their plan. Responsibilities are clear.

A6   Seminar in focus groups

In this activity, a number of tables are arranged in groups, with each table hosting a particular focus for the topic in hand. Learners join tables as directed by the teacher.

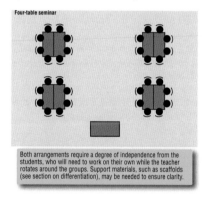

Four-table seminar

Both arrangements require a degree of independence from the students, who will need to work on their own while the teacher rotates around the groups. Support materials, such as scaffolds (see section on differentiation), may be needed to ensure clarity.

This example shows seminars going on involving four focus areas, but a similar arrangement might have three, five or six tables depending upon the number of areas for study chosen by the teacher. There are many ways in which this concept can be used by teachers. Three examples follow.

A7   Focus groups by ability

The teacher arranges topic tables, each hosting a different focus. The difficulty levels of the tasks, however, vary and this provides a good way to differentiate in the allocation to tables.

This arrangement is all about differentiation. In mathematics, for example, the 'cabaret' groups might be required to investigate the same data set, but the tasks or problems involving this data range from the complex to the straightforward. The most confident learner in each group joins others in tackling the complex task and the same structure is used in allocating learners for the other three focus tasks. Teachers or LSAs can join tables to provide support or challenge.

A8   The Jigsaw (or Envoy)

Members of a small group are allocated responsibility for researching one aspect of a topic with others doing the same and then reporting back to their original group.

In this arrangement, each group of four learners (as in the 'cabaret' arrangement above) is required to undertake research on a topic, e.g. Victorian England. The plan is to produce an article for a history magazine. The teacher has defined the headings: *crime, poverty, factories* and *the workhouse*. Each learner is allocated responsibility for one of these (differentiated tasks can be used here) and then, as an '*envoy*', joins learners from the other groups allocated the same research task.

The research on each seminar table can be conducted collaboratively, but each individual must produce a summary sheet (possibly with the support of a scaffold) and then return to their original 'cabaret' group. They then take it in turns to teach the others what they found and a final article is produced for the magazine with contributions from all four learners.

A9   The Circus

Members of small groups rotate around the classroom, undertaking research on different aspects of the same topic. The group finally reconvenes and produces a final report.

This arrangement is like the *Jigsaw* example above, but in the 'circus' each of the four students in the group starts at a different 'seminar' table to do the research. After 15 minutes the teacher blows a whistle and all move to a new table, visiting all four during the lesson. They then regroup for preparing their final report.

A10   You are responsible!

All learners in the group are given a number (e.g. 1–6). A list of questions is produced with a number in brackets, e.g. (1). Learner 1 researches all the 1s, learner 2 researches all the 2s etc.

This technique is particularly useful for watching videos or undertaking research from books or the internet. Differentiation can be applied in allocating numbers and a plenary will involve each group producing a master sheet with all the answers or research findings, with contributions from each member of each group. In the example below, the class has to watch a video on the history of the European Union, and each student in each group of six has two questions to look for and make notes on: one question from early in the video and one from the second half. (For groups of four there would be three questions each.) The final chronology sheet will include findings from all learners.

The European Union

1. Questions	2. Questions	3. Questions
Which Prime Minister first used the phrase United States of Europe?	What year was the Schuman Declaration?	What happened in 1957?
In what year did the Berlin Wall fall?	How many members were there with Enlargement?	Romania and Bulgaria joined in which year?
4. Questions	**5. Questions**	**6. Questions**
What year did the European Community expand?	Which country became a member in 1981?	Which two countries joined in 1986?
What important thing happened in 1999?	Name two things Europe improved in as a result of the Union. Science was one, name two others.	We now have European competitions in sport. Football is one. Name two others.

A11   The Periphery arrangement

The tables are placed around the outside of the classroom with the learners facing the wall.

A table in the middle of the room is used for resources and tutorials.

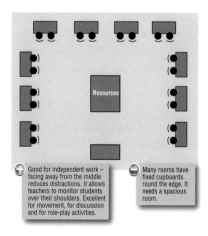

Good for independent work – facing away from the middle reduces distractions. It allows teachers to monitor students over their shoulders. Excellent for movement, for discussion and for role-play activities.

Many rooms have fixed cupboards round the edge. It needs a spacious room.

This arrangement is frequently adopted by teachers where students are working at computer stations. It allows teachers to circulate and see the screens, intervening for support or challenge. It can be used by other teachers and is particularly useful if the learners are spending a significant amount of time working independently. They are facing away from other students and are therefore less likely to be distracted. When the teacher wants whole-class teaching, all learners turn their chairs around and it is easy to form a circle for discussion, debate or circle time. Younger learners can also bring their chairs close to the teacher if, for example, they are about to read together. The periphery arrangement creates space for activities such as role-play and for tutorials in the centre of the room with a small group.

A12   The Boardroom

The tables are arranged either as a rectangle or as three sides of a rectangle in order to facilitate whole-class teaching interspersed with discussion and debate.

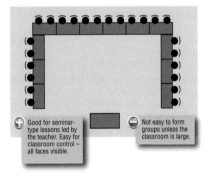

⊕ Good for seminar-type lessons led by the teacher. Easy for classroom control – all faces visible.

⊖ Not easy to form groups unless the classroom is large.

This arrangement is frequently chosen by teachers of academic subjects in post-16 education where lessons are characterised by teacher instruction, note-taking, questioning, discussion and debate. All faces are visible and participation is encouraged because no one student dominates because of where they sit. If teachers want to introduce group activity, it is easy in larger rooms to move chairs to form groups of three or four on either side of the table. This arrangement also supports individual or group presentations.

The boardroom arrangement with a full rectangle of tables also works well for small classes, e.g. a special needs group of 10 or 12 students. When a teacher has a small class in a large classroom, there is often a tendency for learners to be scattered to the four parts of the room. This can create difficulties with classroom control and the boardroom layout is a good alternative.

The teacher, possibly an LSA and the 12 learners sit close together around six tables grouped in a rectangle. It is a very adult way of working and the teacher can not only control behaviour more easily but can generate participation around the table with all learners relatively close to each other. No voices need to be raised and the shy learners feel able to speak with more confidence. I have seen this choice of layout transform the learning experiences of small classes of learners with low confidence.

---

1   All of the images in this section came from *Feedback and Marking: the handbook* by Robert Powell. More information can be found at www.robertpowelltraining.co.uk.

Lesson Planning: the menu

The Purpose of the Lesson

Alternative headings

Lesson aims or objectives

Learning outcomes (LO)

Success criteria

Introduction

Different approaches are used here, but whatever phrase is used, the key aim is for learners to be able to visualise what the lesson is about, what skills or knowledge are to be addressed and what outcomes can be expected to show that learners have made appropriate progress.

Key issues

Some lesson-planning formats require teachers to list 'objectives', 'outcomes' and 'success criteria'. While teachers must follow the guidance issued by their schools or colleges, I would urge leadership teams to be more flexible in their thinking for the following reasons:

- If objectives, outcomes and success criteria are displayed at the beginning of a lesson, what many students see is a mass of words, some of which have no meaning to them. Teachers will lose some students at this early stage.

- 'Objectives' and 'outcomes' are 'teacher' words, and can often be combined in a single phrase such as '*By the end of this lesson you will be able to answer the question why...*' (See B1 below). This has fewer words and will be more accessible to most learners.

- The sharing of '*success criteria*' is an important ingredient – learners need to be able to visualise their journey to success. Sometimes, however, it will be better for the teacher to leave the criteria until later. While the overall purpose of the learning needs to be clear ('where we are going'), it makes no sense to share the details for success criteria at this stage if the actual product (essay, design, investigation etc.) will not be undertaken until the third or fourth lesson.

- Success criteria should be differentiated. The '*all*', '*most*' and '*some*' approach is not recommended, however. To say to a group of learners only 'some' of you will achieve this is misguided; the concept is not aspirational and is likely to produce a self-fulfilling prophecy – only some learners will achieve at a higher level. Alternatives for differentiated lesson aims follow in the main body of the book.

- The purpose of the lesson, whatever format is used, should be visible throughout a lesson or series of lessons. It is helpful to both teachers and learners if it is displayed for reference throughout, and not just flashed up on an interactive whiteboard at the beginning. This is far better than asking learners to copy aims into their books (see below).

- Some leadership teams require learners to copy the displayed 'aims' into their exercise books or folders at the beginning of lessons. This may be necessary on rare occasions (if it is an exam question, for example), but should not be the norm. Copying the aims into books is a monotonous, time-consuming activity that is unlikely to engage the learners at the beginning of a lesson – the very time when good teachers are trying to win over the hearts and minds of the class.

A single lesson or a series of lessons?

The majority of schools and colleges that adopt a lesson-planning format design one for a single lesson. Most teachers deliver units of study that cover more than one lesson – it is quite rare to see a single lesson with a beginning, middle and end. It makes sense, therefore, for the planning process to recognise progression over a number of lessons. Ofsted inspectors in England sensibly now judge progress 'over time' and no longer on a 20-minute snapshot.

A teacher introducing a new topic might, for example, focus on simply engaging the learner with a sense of mystery, intrigue, curiosity or wonder. Such lessons will be the same experience for all and the following lessons will be when observers will see the differentiation, the challenge, the independent or small group investigations, the use of speaking, listening, ICT ... and so on.

A lesson-planning format like the one below shows the progression across four lessons. The arrow shows a visitor where the class is in the sequence. An observer, who might only witness 20 minutes of one lesson, can glance at the last column and see the variety of approaches adopted over the four lessons. In this example, techniques from the menu are in blue.

Lesson	Learning outcomes	Phases of lesson	Resources/Support/homework	Assessment	Skills
1-4	Key question: What animals are endangered, why is this happening and what can be done to protect them? Learners must: > identify which animals are endangered, where they can be found and why they are under threat > list ways that animals can be protected Learners must: > explain why some humans are causing animals to become endangered > identify patterns relating to endangered species Learners could: > evaluate a range of strategies to protect endangered species > produce a manifesto for change	1. Ppt animals (extinct, under threat, fine) decide which 2. Plot endangered animals around the World. 3. Map with numbers 4. Report from homework the causes of animals being endangered. 5. Categorise (habitat, pollution/climate, commercial, hunting) 6. Jigsaw analysis 7. Revisit map and identify patterns (developing countries) 8. Brainstorm ways to protect animals 9. Produce a visual map of strategies 10. Introduce idea of the manifesto 11. Create the manifesto	Scaffold Animals Ppt Fact sheet and map Map with numbers (extension) Enquiry homework with scaffold Visual map Scaffold Visual map (with images) Scaffold Homework- manifesto poster	Oral feedback Peer assessment Formal	Speaking Whole class and paired work Map skills Paired and small groups Speaking and group collaboration Map skills Formal writing skills
	Evaluation				

Starters and plenaries

Readers may be confused as to why the menu does not include major headings for starters and plenaries. There are two main reasons for this.

First, there are simply thousands of starter and plenary activities being used and a handbook of this nature could not contemplate including them all. The app version allows teachers to add a range of starters and plenaries if they choose, and if they have no access to the app they can still add them as an appendix to the handbook using the same coding and key word system.

Second, I have doubts about the whole concept of starters and plenaries as an essential start or finish to a lesson. I have no problem with the argument that lessons should begin with settled classes and a clear focus for the learning, and in some schools and colleges where leadership has identified behaviour as an issue, a clear policy that all lessons begin in a uniform way has much to commend it. But once behaviour issues have been addressed, or in schools and colleges where there are no such problems, the expectation that all lessons begin with a starter and end with a plenary is, I believe, too rigid. Indeed, there are a host of reasons why such a policy will be potentially harmful.

Good lessons start with purpose. In many practical lessons, for example Art, Music, Design and Technology, ICT and a host of vocational courses in Further Education, students arrive ready to continue with their project. Clear purpose for such students comes from the classroom management training of the teacher and from their use of record-keeping and personal logs. What is the purpose of a starter? They know what they are doing and are keen to start. On the occasions when teachers feel a starter is required to build upon the last lesson or to refocus on certain key issues then a starter is a good idea, but this decision should be left to the judgement of the professional.

A more productive policy, I believe, is to adopt a principles' approach[2] where all lessons *must* begin with purpose and regular reviews of progress must take place. The starter and the plenary are then methods of choice used by teachers when appropriate and not a 'rule' for all. A host of other approaches for establishing purpose and for reviewing progress then come into play, some of which will appear in later sections.

A simple statistic shows the benefits in terms of time of a principles' approach. If a school has a six-period day, and starters and plenaries are compulsory, it would mean that over any 5-year period learners have 5700 starters and 5700 plenaries. If each of these averages at 10 minutes each then in any one 38-week academic year, just over 15 weeks are used doing starters and plenaries. Over a 5-year period this is just over 2 years, leaving just 3 years for the main body of learning. And this statistic doesn't take into account the time lost by students in moving between lessons.

---

2. The principles' approach is described in detail in the handbook *Outstanding Teaching, Learning and Assessment*, available from www.robertpowelltraining.co.uk.

B1   Answer questions

By the end of this lesson you will be able to answer the following questions:

- ....
- ....
- ....

The questions might include words such as: What? Why? Who? When? How?
The aims might be displayed on a flipchart or on a 'Magic Whiteboard' (http://www.magicwhiteboard.co.uk/) at the side of the main whiteboard.

B2   Bloom's

By the end of this lesson (or series of lessons) you will be able to:

- Describe...
- List...
- Analyse...
- Compare...
- Evaluate...
- Design...

Bloom's taxonomy is a useful reference point for teachers when planning lessons. It offers a differentiated structure where the verbs chosen show differentiation over time. Learners start off '*listing*', move into '*analysing*', progress to a '*compare and contrast*' phase and end by '*creating*' or '*designing*' their own product.

B3   Must, should, could

By the end of this lesson (or series of lessons) you:

- Must...
- Should...
- Could...

The use of the words 'must', 'should' and 'could' is preferable to 'all, most and some' because the word 'some' is limiting whereas *all* learners '*could*' attempt the task or activity. The key to the use of this approach is in the teacher's head. There must be an *expectation* that all learners will progress towards the higher levels of achievement. The moment either the teacher or the students see the word '*must*' and conclude that this is all they have to do, the approach will fail.

B4   Key questions + headings

The teacher displays at the top of a flipchart questions such as 'What?', 'When?', 'Why?' 'Who?', 'Where?', 'How?' and beneath key headings from the topic.

The example here, from a Victorians topic, might look like this.

What? When? Why? Who? Where? How?

- Slums
- Workhouse
- Factories
- Crime
- Poverty
- Sanitation

The headings can be used for mini plenaries if the teacher examines them in sequence. They can also be used for classroom organisation where small 'focus' groups take responsibility for research on their allocated heading. All groups must use the key question words at the top in their investigations. This 'aims' approach shares the purpose and helps with the classroom management of group work.

B5   Learners ask the questions

Teachers begin by stimulating the students: e.g. images, music, video, role-play, reading or a combination of these. Small groups then meet and the resulting questions are turned into lesson aims.

This approach to sharing purpose can be used by most teachers. The teacher begins by displaying the flipchart as in the example below. The bullet points are blank. The teacher then presents the stimulus after which students in small groups generate series of questions.

For example, a series of lessons on the original Civil Rights Movement in the USA might begin with a PowerPoint displaying a number of images portraying the events that took place (e.g. Rosa Parks, Little Rock High School, the marches, the Ku Klux Klan, segregation in restaurants, King's Washington speech … and so on). The song by Marvin Gaye, *Abraham*, *Martin and John*, plays in the background.

> By the end of these lessons you will be able to answer the following questions:
> * .....
> * .....
> * .....
> * .....
> * .....

Small groups meet and then come back with questions that are then added to the flipchart.

The teacher adds the students' questions to the flipchart. The lesson aims have come from the curiosity of students.

> By the end of these lessons you will be able to answer the following questions:
>
> * Why is there a bus on the slides?
> * Who is that woman being fingerprinted?
> * Why are people marching?
> * What happened to the missing Civil Rights workers?
> * Who is that man making that speech?
> * Who are those people in white cloaks?
> * Why was he shot?

I have worked with teachers planning a similar start on topics such as Victorians, deforestation, training and fitness, the class system, franchises, constructing a house, the Aberfan disaster, endangered animals, chemical reactions and healthy eating. All contained music, and the images selected represented key agendas from the schemes of work.

B6   Mystery lesson

The teacher displays a flipchart with a large question mark in the centre and tells the learners that the aims of the lesson are a mystery and that the plenary will be used for small groups to try and decide what the aims were.

This technique works particularly well when the teacher does not want the students to be 'fed' the learning aims. For example, if the teacher is seeking an emotional response from students from literature, artwork, music, philosophy, or from political or social issues, then a short session at the end of the lesson where they share their emotions can be a really effective learning experience. Displaying aims such as '*By the end of this lesson you will learn how devious Lady Macbeth is*' does not work as well as students voicing this opinion after reading the scene(s) from the play.

The 'mystery lesson' works well with younger learners when the teacher has a list of key learning aims hidden (perhaps with the 'blind' tool on the interactive whiteboard). Small groups of students are asked to see how many of the 'aims' they can list before the teacher reveals them. Students love this competitive activity.

B7   Long-term and short-term aims

Learners in some subjects work over many weeks on the same project and teachers may find it useful to display the long-term aims alongside those for that particular lesson.

When observers visit a lesson where students are working independently on a project, it is often difficult for them to judge how much progress learners are making. Where the students are working on different projects or in different media, they are often required by their teachers to maintain personal logs or diaries (see B8 below).

When, however, the majority of students are at the same stage, working on similar tasks, it is possible for teachers to display the long-term aims alongside the immediate focus for that lesson. The example below is from Design and Technology and on this occasion the purpose is displayed on an interactive whiteboard. The arrow indicates the stage of the production plan. This teacher is using a 'levels' approach but other versions of differentiated outcomes will work just as well.

Production Plan

Week 8
1. Design the graphic in 2d design
2. Apply graphic to board template

Week 9
1. Identify and understand components for electronic dice
2. Solder electronic components to PCB

5

Week 10
1. Design the box net in 2d design
2. Apply the graphic to the net
3. Cut the box out using the CAM1

Week 11
1. Final assembly of all components
2. Design and make themed accessories such as counters

Today's Outcomes

Level 4
Identify and state the electronic components needed in your circuit when soldering.

Level 5
Explain and demonstrate the function of each component.

Level 6
Assemble the circuit correctly and safely, being aware of Health and Safety rules.

B8   Aims from learner logs or diaries

The learning aims in some subjects and courses may be different for each student, and in such cases personal logs or diaries are a means of starting lessons with clear purpose.

The specifications and assessment criteria of some courses require learners to work independently on long-term projects, often with a personalised focus. Music and ICT are two examples. Students in performing arts will often be working in different media, independently or in groups, and they will often keep personal logs of tasks, activities, feedback and achievements. One of the ways teachers can start such a lesson is to ask learners to open their logs, showing personalised learning aims. The Excel spreadsheet below comes from a music department. The record is maintained by the student and contains columns for feedback and a hyperlink column where a recording of the composition in its various stages can be listened to by observers as a check on progress. (More details on this are included in Section G on assessment and feedback.)

B9   Visual map or overview

A visual map or overview of the topic with visual clues will help students of all ages and abilities to see the context for each lesson and help them to see the connections between different aspects of the topic.

Consider the two versions of learning aims below on the topic of healthy living.

Fit and Healthy

In this unit students will learn:
- how the human respiratory, digestive and circulatory systems interact to maintain activity
- about the functions of the skeleton
- about ways in which diet, exercise, smoking and drugs affect health

students should learn:
- that a balanced diet requires nutrients, including vitamins, in the correct quantities
- that deficiencies in specific nutrients lead to specific diseases
- how evidence about specific nutrient deficiencies is used.

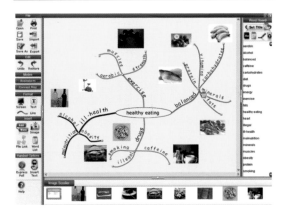

The complex text version may create anxiety for poor readers or EAL learners and has no visual clues to the meanings of the technical terms. The visual version provides a more accessible sense of purpose to the learners and visual clues to the meaning of technical terms. It will be accompanied by key questions. '*You will be able to answer the following questions: What is a balanced diet and how…*' The visual map can be printed out and pasted into folders or exercise books and students can even annotate it as they progress through the course. It can also become a revision map if the course has final tests or examinations.

The software used allows students to participate in the creation of the map by suggesting which words and images should be dragged out from the side or bottom bars to connect with major headings. (The EyeWrite software can be found at www.robertpowelltraining.co.uk.)

Lesson Planning: the menu

Engaging Learners

Alternative headings

Fascinators

Hooks

Introduction

Most teachers will agree that a good start to a lesson creates the climate for real engagement, motivation and participation. Conversely, a poor start can be rectified, but more often it can dent the confidence of the teacher and lead to an uphill battle in winning the hearts and minds of the students.

Key issues

Outstanding lessons don't just happen. The foundations put in place beforehand by skilled teachers contribute greatly to the success of the learners, so while this section examines engagement, it must draw attention to the other key ingredients of outstanding practice.

- **Classroom management**

  Seating plans, ground rules, ethos, displays (e.g. key words) are all important if a good start to a lesson with high student engagement is to materialise.

- **Differentiation**

  If there is a wide range of skills or confidence in the class, the differentiation strategies employed will have a huge influence on the level of engagement.

- **Widespread participation**

  Achieving high levels of participation right from the first few moments of a lesson is essential – *start as you mean to go on* is an important rule to remember.

- **Success**

  Don't go for the jugular too early. I always advise teachers new to the profession to start lessons with *success for all*. It is very easy to increase the challenge early in the lesson, but if you start from the familiar, make everyone feel confident, then students take up the challenge in good heart. Start too high and you may have a very quiet classroom.

- **Passion**

  The most important ingredient of all, however, is teachers' passion and enthusiasm for what they are teaching. The energy that comes from such teachers communicates to learners, and I urge all young teachers starting their careers never to lose their passion. That is why most leadership teams are striving to address the workload issues and why, in my opinion, they must be flexible in their guidance to teachers on lesson planning. Highly rigid structures produce straitjackets and suffocate individuality.

C1   Learning begins on arrival

An activity is prepared ready for students to start the moment they walk into the room. The teacher does not wait for late arrivals and the activity stops soon after all the learners have arrived.

The purpose of this technique is to engage the learners as soon as they walk into the room. When the latecomers arrive, the activity will cease and the teacher will review the learning. In the example below, the image is on the whiteboard as learners walk in.

Find the hazards

Any kind of image or media can be used and this will be effective in most subjects and with most age groups. Sometimes it can be used to reflect upon previous learning, but it can also be used to develop curiosity for a new topic. A stimulating image or media and some good questions are all that is required.

Some interactive whiteboards have a 'tickertape' facility where the questions scroll across the screen. This is particularly effective here.

C2   Snippets

The teacher gives students a taster or overview of what is to come, stimulating their curiosity.

This can be done in many ways: a collage of images or photographs; a set of headlines that engage and stimulate; extracts from the texts that will be used later; intriguing questions that have to be answered or solved.

I was privileged to witness an example of this approach in a special needs department of a college where the numeracy teacher was introducing counting in the units of money. She began the lesson not by introducing these aims, but by telling the students that they were going to open a healthy eating stall for a week in order to raise funds for charity. The students would run the shop and sell fruit such as apples, oranges, carrots and grapes along with low-calorie snacks. But before they could do that they had to learn to count and give change in the units of money. The engagement was instant and they threw themselves into the numeracy tasks with palpable enthusiasm.

C3 You ask the questions (see B5)

C4 Lesson 'trailer'

The teacher introduces a topic in such a way that the learners are desperate to find out more. It can be seen rather like a trailer for a film.

One of the best trailers I saw was by a teacher of English who was beginning the topic '*how do authors engage the reader?*' He began by reading to his class the opening paragraphs of a range of novels and short stories, all selected because of their brilliant opening pages. Not only did the learners engage in the analysis activity that followed, '*what engaged you?*', but the school library was inundated with requests for the books used in the lesson. They wanted more!

C5 Start with a problem

This technique also involves intrigue. The teacher introduces one or more problems and tells the learners that the purpose of the coming lessons is for them to try and solve whichever problem they are given.

This approach can be effective with most subjects and age groups. I have seen it used in science, design and technology, humanities, mathematics, sport, health, modern foreign languages and ICT in both primary and secondary, and in a host of vocational courses post-16.

One example was a series of lessons in geography focusing on endangered animals. The teacher began by showing a PowerPoint with 14 endangered animals, with the Elton John song *Circle of Life* from The Lion King playing in the background. She then told the class that they were going to elect an MP for animals who would set up a campaign to save them. To do this each group would have to produce a manifesto before the mock election. The problem was '*how to save the animals*' and the product was the manifesto.

C6   Start with the end product

This technique involves the teacher showing the learners examples of the end product that they will be working towards during the coming lessons.

This is closely related to the example above, C2, but works particularly well in courses involving making, doing or designing. For example, PE teachers might ask an older student to demonstrate a somersault on a trampoline, a teacher of music might play a composition from a previous student, and a teacher of Art might show new students an exhibition from last year's class. The key is to engender an '*I can do that*' emotion in the learners and a picture in their heads of where the journey will take them.

C7   Start with the answer

This technique is most often used in mathematics and numeracy. The teacher provides the answer and the learners have to work out the question.

In one junior school classroom I saw a 7-year-old produce 34 questions leading to the answer 11, including a number of negative numbers. The key point of the activity is that it motivates most learners and involves some deeper thinking skills.

I observed a teacher of French apply this technique. She displayed a street map on the screen and provided a range of answers: *l'école*; *la banque*; *le stade*; *l'église* etc. Learners were asked to be town guides and provide directions in French to imaginary tourists. The directions should take them to one of the answers, e.g. *l'école*. In order to do this they had to use phrases such as *à côté de*, *à droite*, *à gauche* and *troisième*. The differentiation was superb. Each student was given a different starting point on the map, with the more confident students given more challenging routes to their allocated destination.

C8   Issue a challenge!

This technique involves the teacher issuing, at the beginning of a lesson, a public challenge for learners to go beyond normal progress and aim for the 'exceptional'.

A brilliant way to motivate learners is to set them a public challenge. The trick for teachers is to match the level of challenge to the learners. If the task is too easy it will create boredom. If it is too challenging there is a danger of learners becoming anxious. Carol Dweck's work on *growth mindsets*[3] emphasises the need for teachers to create a classroom ethos where resilience and 'having a go' without fear of failure are critical if such a challenge is to be taken on with enthusiasm. If this ethos is established, 'issue a challenge' can be a regular feature of a teacher's repertoire.

I supported one primary school teacher in preparing a lesson that was to be observed by the Headteacher as part of the performance management process. In earlier lessons that week he had shown and modelled examples of outstanding descriptive writing, ranging from the old NC Level 2 to Level 6. He chose the descriptive writing theme for his observed lesson with a group of 10-year-olds.

He decided to set them the challenge of editing a piece of writing to transform it from Level 2 to Level 5 or 6. He issued the challenge and then showed them a vivid photograph of a destitute child from Victorian England. He instructed the learners all to write a poor Level 2 description of this child. When this was done, he asked all the learners to swop books with their peer partners and then to rewrite their friend's work to achieve at least a Level 5 and, if possible, a Level 6. Not only did he achieve a Grade 1 lesson in his feedback from the Headteacher, but all of the learners authored a Level 5 or 6 for their redrafted descriptions, including learners whose previous work was below such levels. He also was delighted with the enthusiasm the challenge had generated; the excitement when he issued the challenge was clearly visible in the eyes and demeanour of the learners.

C9 Ensure clarity

This technique is critical. Ensure that all learners are clear about the purpose of the learning, have access to the key vocabulary and understand what they have to do if there is to be a period of independent or small group activity.

This issue is dealt with in more detail in other sections: *Purpose of the lesson, Differentiation* and *Success criteria*. But it needs to be emphasised here that teachers will be unable to engage and motivate learners if they are not clear what they are supposed to be doing. Lack of clarity creates anxiety and with anxiety other behaviours such as restlessness, inattention and other forms of low-level disruption.

3   Dweck, Carol (2007), *Mindset: The New Psychology of Success* (New York, Ballantine).

Literacy and Language

Alternative headings

Building language

Key vocabulary

Introduction

The issue of language should be on the lesson-planning agenda of most teachers, regardless of subject, level or target age group. Using spoken and written language well is often high on the list of criteria for the top grades.

Understanding and applying technical vocabulary accurately and with confidence are often the hallmark of a high-performing student. On the other hand, any deficiency in language is often a cause of learner anxiety, and extended into society there is a high correlation between poor levels of literacy and all the indices of deprivation, crime, unemployment and ill-health.

Key issues

The phrase literacy and language covers a wide range of issues, some of which will be examined in the menu that follows.

- **Key vocabulary**

  Every subject or topic will have a set of key words that provide the foundation stones for understanding. Teachers need to identify such words in their planning and help learners to master them.

- **Widening vocabulary**

  Numerous studies have shown the link between a rich vocabulary and academic, social and career success.

- **Developing writing skills**

  Most academic examinations assess knowledge and skills through written assessments, and in wider society writing skills are valued in and out of the workplace. Studies show, on the other hand, that only 50% of the prison population can write up to the level of a 10-year-old child.

- **Reading**

  Being able to read is a prerequisite for learners who want to access the vast majority of the school and college curriculum. Failure to master this skill can lead to lifelong esteem problems and other social ills; 80% of the prison population read at or below the level of a 10-year-old child. In addition, 70% of students excluded permanently from school have weak literacy skills.

- **Developing speaking and listening skills**

  Speaking skills are rarely assessed in academic examinations, although in modern foreign languages and a range of vocational courses they form part of the standard assessments. Nevertheless, spoken skills are valued by most teachers in most subjects; indeed, many teachers will admit to making judgements about students based on their contributions or otherwise in oral work and questioning.

- **The teaching of reading**

  This book will not include a menu for the teaching of reading. This is a highly skilled and specialised activity, whether with young children or adult learners, and not one that lends itself to this menu approach for lesson planning.

D1 Identify and display key technical terms

Technical terms related to the subject or topic have been identified and displayed.

At the beginning of topics, teachers often introduce learners to new vocabulary or concepts and it helps if the teacher can point to such terms on a poster or display. On occasions, images may be attached to aid understanding and memory. The words on display should be large enough for easy reference and referred to during teacher instruction. If they are on the wall but not mentioned, they are simply decoration that will have little impact. The presence of the display will allow the teacher to revisit key concepts in the following lessons, e.g. by pointing at the display and saying 'which word am I referring to?'

The visualisation of words can help EAL learners – teachers of modern foreign languages have always adopted a multi-sensory approach to vocabulary. I remember seeing a French lesson where the young teacher was acting out a bad back while repeating the phrase 'J'ai mal au dos'. When the learners did the writing later in the lesson, there were various spellings of the word 'dos' – 'dow', 'dough' and 'doe' among them. They had heard the word but not seen it.

D2 Display of adjectives, adverbs, nouns, verbs and connectives

Contextualised adjectives, nouns, verbs, adverbs and connectives can also be displayed as a means of widening vocabulary and encouraging more complex language structures.

Adjectives

brave, courageous, scared, clever, large, strong, beautiful, wicked, small, scary, greedy, vain, helpful, nasty, selfish, dark, kind, rough, hard, smelly, confusing, lost, hopeful, funny, sad, violent, heroic, vicious, longing, isolated, alone, huge, tiny, agile, noble, ferocious, sinister, cunning

This adjectives box, displayed while studying the topic of Greek Myths, was accompanied by one for nouns, adverbs, verbs and connectives. During their work on the end product, an imaginary review of Theseus and the Minotaur for the local newspaper, all learners used words from the posters to improve their final assessments.

D3 Words with scores

The teacher displays key words and adds scores to them, encouraging learners to achieve as high a score as possible.

Adjectives

eerie[5], sombre[6], deathly[4], haunted[3], sinister[5], horrifying[5], dark[3], scary[3], terrifying[4], terrible[4], ghoulish[6], macabre[6], nasty[3], ominous[6], spooky[5], alarming, apprehensive[6], chilling[5], fearful[4], frightening[4], frightful[5], ghostly[4], wicked[4], musty, damp, icy[3], vicious[5]

In this writing project on the theme of the Haunted House, learners chose words like 'frightful' and 'apprehensive' to improve their scores and their levels. The idea can be applied to most subjects and can include the use of scores for technical terms and higher-level thinking-skills terms such as '*justify*' '*evaluate*' and '*compare and contrast*'. In the example below, the same approach was used to encourage the use of more interesting connectives in a French lesson.

Connectives

et[1], mais[2], donc[3], néanmoins[6], alors[4], pourtant[5], cependant[5], parce que[2], car[2], désormais[6], par contre[5], en plus[5], en fait[4], enfin[3], d'abord[3], ensuite[3], puis[3], deuxièmement[4], à mon avis[4], quant à moi[6], selon moi[5]

d'un côté...d'autre côté[7]

D4   Key words on playing cards

Key words are printed/pasted onto playing cards and used for card games designed to build understanding of technical vocabulary.

Teachers can organise short 'brain breaks' where the learners play in pairs using the cards. Games such as *Whist* take only a few minutes and work well. The key word and its definition are on one side of the card. Learners win cards by correctly defining the word read out by opponents. Snap can also be used – where they match a card with another from the same set (e.g. *both alkalis*).

The game of *Pairs* is enjoyable – where they match a word and a picture. *Word Dominoes* can also be played on cards, and here learners have to try and line up a number of cards, with each word or image on the dominoes correctly linked to the adjacent one. When this is done in small groups, it encourages lots of dialogue and debate, with all the discussion about the *meaning* of words and how they *relate* to another in the same set.

D5   Software for learning words

A wide range of software is available for developing language and vocabulary including games, picture dictionaries and visual planners with key words and images (see B9).

D6   Glossaries

Teachers ask learners to include in their exercise books or folders glossaries of key terms, either provided by the teacher or produced by the students themselves.

D7   Mastery groups for key words

The teacher asks cabaret groups (see A4) to revise key words and then tests them. The total scores of the group are added. The aim is to achieve 'mastery' (100%) through peer coaching.

D8   Scaffolds and models for writing

A range of scaffolds or models from the highly structured to simple 'prompts' can be used to support learners who find it difficult to start or plan writing. (See Section F on differentiation.)

D9   Deeper learning through writing

Learners are asked to use key words or technical terms in a form of writing that will both demonstrate and deepen understanding of those terms.

Low-level writing tasks – e.g. *complete the sentence, fill in the missing words* – can often be completed by students with little understanding; the key terms will be forgotten as soon as the task is over. Deeper tasks can be planned where the learners have to show understanding through their use of the terms. For example, in a lesson on healthy eating learners might be asked to write the script of a conversation (or a letter, editorial, fact sheet) between a doctor and a patient where the doctor is explaining to the patient why he/she needs to reduce high levels of cholesterol.

The key to this task is the use of technical terms. So the task has clear guidance: '*You must use the following terms in your conversation: cholesterol, fibre, saturated fats, salt, arteries, heart disease, strokes, blocking, HDL, atherosclerosis, angina, fatty acids…*' This approach can also be used for oral presentations and can be applied in most subjects and with most ages and levels.

D10   Give us a clue

A fun activity where all learners study a document and then write clues to information, e.g. the name of a character, event, etc. for others to find; great for reading, listening and thinking.

This activity can be used in almost any subject where learners have to read for understanding. The learners' clues must not include the names of people or events or the technical terms that might be the subject of the clues. So in an MfL lesson it might be clues to a family tree or directions on a map, in English it might be clues to a character or a poem, in Habitats it might be clues to a predator or species, in Construction clues to the type of trench being excavated, in History clues to an event or treaty, in Geography clues to a country, city or type of rock, in Art clues to a genre or artist.

The possibilities are endless. The key is to ask students to read, develop the understanding and then deepen the learning by creating clues. Some groups of students will start to use cryptic clues and thinking skills will also be enhanced.

Lesson Planning: the menu

Questioning

Alternative headings

Assessment for Learning (AfL)

Deeper understanding

Introduction

Effective questioning techniques will be examined in this section under two headings: (1) questioning to check understanding, part of the AfL agenda and (2) questioning to deepen and consolidate understanding.

1. Questioning to check understanding (AfL)

Key issues

- **Participation**

  All teachers use questioning to check understanding, and for this to be effective they need widespread participation from learners. A feature of outstanding lessons is the learners' high level of participation. This will be evident when the teacher is questioning the class, when the students are invited to ask questions and when the learners are invited to offer ideas or thoughts on the topic being studied. On the other hand, less successful lessons are characterised by low levels of participation in both thinking and speaking. In such classes, the majority of learners are reluctant to either answer or ask questions and contribute to discussion only when the teacher directs a question at them by name. In such situations, questioning to check understanding is fraught with difficulties. How many learners have responded? What are the silent ones thinking? Is it safe to move on with the lesson when only a few learners have revealed their understanding?

- **Teachers' response to questioning**

  If questioning is to be used by teachers to check understanding, they must be prepared to adapt their teaching in the light of the responses they get from learners. If questioning reveals a widespread lack of understanding, a rethink of the lesson plan is essential with a period of revision being one of the options. If, on the other hand, questioning reveals a degree of mastery from the majority of students, then the lesson plan needs to be adapted to introduce a greater level of challenge. When questioning reveals a mixed response, with a mixture of *mastery*, *basic understanding* and *confusion*, then more complex solutions are called for – see the section on differentiation for ideas on this.

- **Hands-up or no hands-up**

  Teachers the world over will debate the issue of
  who answers questions – '*volunteers*' or
  '*conscripts*'? Strong views are expressed by some
  on this subject, but professional educators will
  make their own decisions and it may be that the
  answer is 'it depends...' There is no doubt that
  some learners in some classes get frustrated if they
  are denied the opportunity of giving the teacher an
  answer. However, there are learners, either because
  of shyness or mental truancy, who never want to
  answer questions and are relieved if the hands-up
  brigade are allowed to dominate questioning
  sessions. A 'mixed economy' is, of course, an
  option, and I am sure there are many teachers who
  use a wide variety of techniques rather than being
  philosophically rooted to a single strategy. Some of
  these options are explored in the menu that follows.

E1   Pre- and post-testing

This technique involves a teacher using a test at the beginning of a topic to assess the degree of prior learning and another at intervals or the end to demonstrate progress.

This technique is particularly useful at the beginning of a course or on transfer between phases or classes, when the teacher does not have trustworthy data on the levels of prior learning in the class. At its simplest, the early test provides feedback to the teacher, allowing the teaching programme to be planned to meet the identified needs. Further tests can be used at intervals in order to check understanding and also to provide positive feedback to learners on the progress they are making or to alert the teacher if such progress is not evident.

E2   Start from the familiar

Participation levels will be enhanced if teachers start with the familiar – questions that most learners can access and respond to, ensuring a few moments of success for all.

If teachers ask really challenging questions in the first few minutes of a questioning session, the majority of learners are likely to freeze with anxiety. It will be very hard to recover from this and the likelihood is that only a few students will participate with any enthusiasm. When the early questions are familiar, however, there is widespread success and opportunities for praise. This breeds confidence, allowing teachers to increase the level of challenge, with learners more likely to participate.

E3   Questions based on Bloom's taxonomy

Bloom's taxonomy is a useful starting point for questions designed to check understanding. The hierarchy of questions can be displayed as a classroom aid.

The display of Bloom's taxonomy can help teachers and learners. Not only do the verbs help teachers to formulate AfL questions, they provide stimulus for learners once teachers make use of questions generated by students in peer questioning.

Learning based on Bloom's Taxonomy - used for outcomes and in AFL

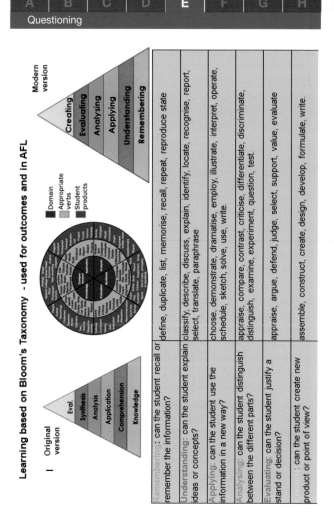

Original version

Modern version

Domain
Appropriate verbs
Student products

	Appropriate verbs
Remembering: can the student recall or remember the information?	define, duplicate, list, memorise, recall, repeat, reproduce state
Understanding: can the student explain ideas or concepts?	classify, describe, discuss, explain, identify, locate, recognise, report, select, translate, paraphrase
Applying: can the student use the information in a new way?	choose, demonstrate, dramatise, employ, illustrate, interpret, operate, schedule, sketch, solve, use, write.
Analysing: can the student distinguish between the different parts?	appraise, compare, contrast, criticise, differentiate, discriminate, distinguish, examine, experiment, question, test.
Evaluating: can the student justify a stand or decision?	appraise, argue, defend, judge, select, support, value, evaluate
Creating: can the student create new product or point of view?	assemble, construct, create, design, develop, formulate, write.

Early questions such as 'list' can quickly be developed into 'describe' and escalated into 'criticise' and 'distinguish'. Higher-level questioning is examined in the second half of this section.

E4   Show-me boards

Wider participation in answering questions is achieved if teachers ask learners to record their answers on show-me boards, which they display simultaneously.

When teachers want to check levels of understanding, some will use a 'hands-up' approach with volunteers, some will select the learners they want to answer, and some will use a randomised system of nomination. In a large class, only five or six learners may be questioned and the use of show-me boards for some types of questioning will provide 100% participation; and if the boards are all displayed at the same moment, the level of understanding across the class is much easier to assess.

E5 Randomised questioning

The teacher uses a randomising system to decide which student will answer each question. Some teachers use lollipop sticks while others prefer electronic systems.

Rather than ask for 'hands-up', teachers can randomise which learner answers. Some teachers list all the class names on an individual lollipop stick in a jar. The question is asked, 20 seconds of thinking time is given, and then the teacher takes a stick from the jar with the name of the learner who must answer. (Do not take out the stick before asking the question – if you do, only one person will then think over the question!) The lollipop system has its problems (e.g. storing lots of jars when the teacher has 10 different classes), so teachers may prefer to use an electronic system. Randomising can be achieved in PowerPoint. Simply create a slide and insert a photograph that links to the theme of the lesson. Copy the slide to match the number of learners in the class (e.g. 30.).

Now add a text box to each page and type in the name of each learner, one per page. In PowerPoint now select the transition between slides and set it to 0.00 seconds. In the Slide Show option, select 'loop continuously'. You are ready to use randomisation. Click on the 'S' key on your keyboard and the slides loop at a very fast pace. Press 'S' again and the slides stop at a name. This learner must answer. When you are ready, press 'S' again and repeat each time you want a new name on the screen. Another 'fruit machine' electronic version of randomised names can be found free of charge at www.classtools.net.

E6   Support Groups

Wide participation can be achieved through small groups where individuals think of their answers before 'pooling' them to the Scribe who lists their answers and records names.

Support groups are described in more detail in section (F) on differentiation, and the role of the Scribe and the recording method are explained in A5. When teachers use this technique, more learners are involved and even the shy or reticent have an opportunity for their answers to be listed. The teacher will ask the Scribe in each group to provide an answer, checking how many other groups had the same one. Teachers can, if they wish, say 'great answer; who suggested it?'

E7   Electronic response systems

Electronic response systems allow teachers to get 100% response from learners. Some provide named responses and instant analysis to show the levels of understanding.

A range of learner response systems are available and some have moved beyond the 'clicker' mentality, where all questions were multiple choice and users simply clicked a number or letter to record their answer or opinion. The most sophisticated technology is Promethean's *ActivExpression*, which allows learners to respond in a variety of ways.

A range of multiple-choice options are provided but learners can also respond with text, number, true/false or rank in order. Instant analysis is provided with output to Excel. Teachers who use such technology get instant feedback on levels of understanding, allowing them to modify lessons in line with the assessment information. *ActivExpression* also provides a 'live' feedback option, which will be explained in the section on Assessment for Learning (G15).

Smart's *Quizdom* performs all the functions above apart from the live feedback option. Both systems will work in any classroom, regardless of the type of interactive whiteboard being used. It is also possible, but currently more challenging to implement, for electronic responses to be made from personal devices including mobile phones. There is no doubt that this facility will become easier to establish in the near future.

2. Questioning to deepen and consolidate understanding

Key issues

- Most teachers at some point will want to move beyond a simple check on understanding into deeper learning and consolidation, and questioning is one of the techniques that will do this. While a quick check on understanding might be accomplished in a few minutes, deeper questioning requires more time and greater involvement of the learners and as such might be used as one of the major activities of a lesson.

- Some of the techniques that follow will make use of groups and the choice over what type of group (e.g. focus group, ability group, Jigsaw group) will depend upon the purpose of the activity. Deeper questioning can be used earlier in a unit of work to deepen understanding or towards the end to deepen and consolidate understanding. When teachers use groups for questioning, as in some of the examples in the menu that follows, it pays to have invested some time in training learners for their role in group activity, issues which were examined in Section A on classroom organisation.

- Most questioning in classrooms is dominated by teachers' questions. Teachers who invite learners to ask the questions, and have practised this process with them, often find that the questions are more challenging than the questions they would have asked themselves. Techniques for this are included below.

E8 Questions based on Bloom's Taxonomy

The higher levels of Bloom's will be used to deepen understanding, with verbs such as *compare*, *evaluate*, *formulate*, *defend* and *construct* at the heart of the questioning.

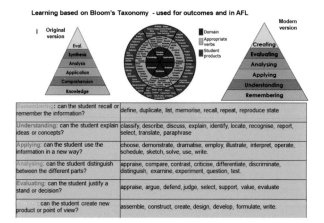

Learning based on Bloom's Taxonomy - used for outcomes and in AFL

Remembering: can the student recall or remember the information?	define, duplicate, list, memorise, recall, repeat, reproduce state
Understanding: can the student explain ideas or concepts?	classify, describe, discuss, explain, identify, locate, recognise, report, select, translate, paraphrase
Applying: can the student use the information in a new way?	choose, demonstrate, dramatise, employ, illustrate, interpret, operate, schedule, sketch, solve, use, write.
Analysing: can the student distinguish between the different parts?	appraise, compare, contrast, criticise, differentiate, discriminate, distinguish, examine, experiment, question, test.
Evaluating: can the student justify a stand or decision?	appraise, argue, defend, judge, select, support, value, evaluate
: can the student create new product or point of view?	assemble, construct, create, design, develop, formulate, write.

E9 Pose, pause, bounce, pounce

This technique involves teachers bouncing answers from one learner to the next, increasing the challenge each time; no *hands-up* – the teacher selects the learners who will respond.

Dylan Wiliam refers to this technique and highlights its benefits. First, the teacher must pause after asking a question. Too many teachers, he claims, worried at a lack of response, jump in too early after asking a question without giving sufficient thinking and reflection time.

Second, the teacher selects who answers (Student A) and that learner's response is bounced to another student (Student B), pounced on by the teacher who throws an additional prompt such as '*give me an example of what (student A) means by…*'. This technique depends upon deeper questioning and all learners must concentrate hard because no one knows who will have to respond next.

E10 Answer and pass

In this activity the teacher selects the learner who must respond and then selects another to follow up the previous answer with *'I agree/disagree with that answer because…'*.

This technique also demands a high level of concentration because each learner chosen (and the random methods can be used here) must make some kind of comment on the previous learner's response before offering their own answer or thoughts. Teachers might like to display a poster with appropriate connectives, like in the example below, to support learners in the process.

I agree with G… because…

I do not agree with G… because…

P…'s idea is great and I would like to add the fact that…

While S… makes a good point about …, there is another issue that needs to be examined…

D… suggests that….. I support that but think you also have to consider…

F… makes a valid point, but where is the evidence for…

E11 Discussion questions

In this activity, teachers post a key question and invite groups of students to agree one positive response, one negative response and one question that needs to be addressed.

This is rather like the Cort Thinking PMI activity, *Plus*, *Minus and Interesting*. So, for example, the question *'Would a move to Chinese-style education improve learning outcomes?'* is posted on the wall. (The teacher might have produced a handout or shown a video with information on this topic.) Small groups are now asked to produce one positive response and one negative response, both with reasons, and one 'interesting' question that needs to be answered before a final answer is agreed. The groups report back and their questions are allocated to other groups to consider. This process allows even shy learners to share their opinions and to ask and answer deep questions.

E12   Question prompts for peer questioning

Using Bloom's taxonomy, teachers can improve the level of peer questioning by displaying question prompts on posters.

When teachers want to use peer questioning, they may find learners opting for low-level, closed questions. In order to encourage higher-level questioning, teachers might find it useful, certainly in the early stages, to display question prompts on posters as in the example below.

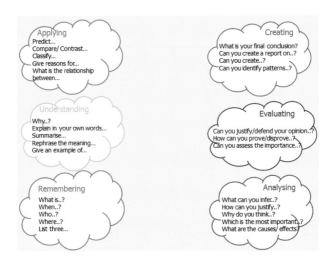

Prompts posters can be very useful in most areas of the curriculum and with most age groups. They are very useful in numeracy and mathematics with questions such as *What happens if we ...? What is the same or different? Can you see a pattern? What do think comes next? How can this pattern help you? Why did you use that method? How else could it be done?*

Teachers of modern foreign languages will also find a prompts poster displaying a range of language structures will stimulate learners to make use of higher-order questions – *justifying, expressing opinions* and *evaluating* as well as encouraging learners to use a range of tenses – *will, have, could, might,* and so on. Poster prompts are also vital when teachers want learners to undertake *self-evaluation* and reflect upon their own work or performance. The use of poster prompts for this agenda will be examined later in the section on feedback.

E13   Peer questioning with scores

When peer questions are generated, teachers can place them on post-it notes on a pin board or poster and ask learners to select a question to answer.

If teachers want to increase the challenge, they can score each question that is created by the learners (e.g. 1–6), with the higher-order ones gaining more points. Learners then choose, or are prompted or directed by the teacher to choose, questions that will move them on from whatever their starting points are. In revision activities, teachers can even make it more fun by selecting appropriate pairs of learners and asking them to challenge each other. If one of the pair selects a 4-point question and answers it correctly, she/he scores 4 points. If it is not correct, the challenger who set the question scores 4.

E14   Graphing peer questions

The process of peer questioning with increasing levels of challenge works well if the teacher places the questions produced by learners on a graph with the most challenging at the top.

This activity is a variation on the scoring technique (E13). Learners will give their questions to the teacher who will place them on the graph by theme (as in the example on Civil Rights below) with the most challenging questions towards the top. Learners then choose or are directed to other learners' questions. Teachers will find that many learners want to have a go at the more complex questions. This can also be conducted using Jigsaw groups (A8) where individuals from the group each take responsibility for one of the questions in the theme they are allocated.

The placing of questions on a whiteboard is made easier if teachers have access to the *Magic Whiteboard* sheets that simply stick to flat surfaces like cling film. They can be wiped for using time and again, and are available in various sizes from flipchart size to A5. They are available from: www.magicwhiteboard.co.uk or Rymans' stationery stores.

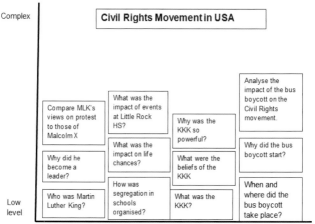

Themes related to the Civil Rights Movement

E15 Peer questioning in Question Time

This is a consolidation activity at the end of a topic when one small group is given the role of 'experts' or the Question Time panel, and other groups prepare questions for them.

This activity rarely fails to motivate learners. The rules are quite clear. The experts spend a short time (e.g. 10 minutes) revising the topic and agreeing who will answer what type of question (they must all take it in turns to answer). The other groups spend the time preparing questions, and in preparing questions they must also prepare answers – they are not allowed to ask questions unless they can answer themselves. The teacher will circulate checking this. When teachers use Question Time they nearly always find the questioning groups will try to create the hardest questions possible; they go for the jugular! If used in conjunction with a questions poster (E12), they will almost certainly opt for the higher-order questions.

The key point of this activity is that the students who learn the most from this process are those who asked the questions. Most teachers who dominate questioning are missing a trick; creating good questions along with the answers is a brilliant learning activity.

E16   Pass the Question

Here, individual learners prepare a question at the top of a folded page with the answer below. The teacher then tears off the question part and allocates it to another learner.

The clear benefit of Pass the Question is differentiation. Once teachers approve the learners' questions and answers, they tear off the top of the page and allocate the question to another learner, taking into account the difficulty level. The more challenging questions go to the most confident, the less challenging to those finding it difficult. The learners who set the question then mark the answers once their peer partners have completed them. Once again, learners strive to make their questions as difficult as possible.

Lesson Planning: the menu

Differentiation in the Classroom

Alternative headings

Personalisation

Meeting the needs of individuals

Challenge and support

Key issues

- **Definitions**

  The term 'differentiation' causes confusion with some teachers because definitions of the concept vary so widely. To some, 'differentiation' is another term for 'special educational needs'. Others widen this definition to include the needs of the most able. For the purposes of this handbook, however, the definition will be: '*interventions that are designed to meet the needs of individual learners*'.

  Therefore, the menu that follows will suggest a range of techniques for meeting individual needs within the mainstream classroom. These 'needs' will include not only those students with learning difficulties or those who need challenge, but the shy, those lacking confidence, those with gaps in prior learning and those whose first language is different to the language used in the class.

  It will *not* include techniques for severe or specific learning difficulties, medical conditions or disabilities. While some of the ideas that follow in the menu may be relevant to such learners, these are specialist areas and not the focus of this handbook.

- **Grouping by ability as a form of differentiation**

  There are teachers who believe that the organisation of learners into classes grouped by ability is itself a form of differentiation. There is no doubt that a narrower range of ability in a class can make differentiation easier to manage – e.g. if the learners are all good readers – but grouping by ability does not make all the learners homogenous.

  The process of setting is not a science – learners might scrape into a top set or just miss out – and the range of skill in any group will depend upon how large the cohort is. An eight-form school organised by ability will have a narrower range in each class than a four-form or two-form entry school. In junior schools, the age difference within any one class may be 11 months and very small schools sometimes have a two-year range in a single class. In any class there will still be a range of needs – the 'gifted' learners who finish before anyone else, the shy learners who never volunteer or the learners with 'blind spots' on particular topics.

- **Differentiation by 'outcome'**

There are teachers who claim that they differentiate 'by outcome'. They set the same task for all learners and allow them to produce their own 'outcomes'. This is not differentiation. Asking students to work on exactly the same learning activity with no intervention of any kind from the teacher is simply poor teaching.

Fortunately, most teachers who use this phrase do intervene, and some clarification is needed to unravel this puzzle. If a teacher sets the same task to all the learners, e.g. a piece of creative writing, and then allows them to proceed through the task without intervention, then this would be poor practice unless the task was some kind of formal assessment where intervention is forbidden.

Most teachers, however, would use a range of interventions. They might set different targets for individuals, they might use a range of scaffolds, they or teaching assistants might spend time in dialogue with individuals, supporting or challenging them, they might use peer assessment of drafts to improve the writing or they might direct individuals to look at modelled examples.

The phrase 'differentiation by outcome' is misleading in most cases and needs to be deleted from teachers' vocabulary. Teachers who claim to use differentiation by 'outcome' perform a disservice to their profession.

Key issues (cont.)

- **Differentiation and lesson plan templates**

  The definition of differentiation used earlier was '*interventions to meet the needs of individuals*'. If that definition is accepted, then it is clear that differentiation impacts upon most aspects of classroom practice: how the classroom ethos is set to make it a safe and welcoming environment; how the environment is designed to stimulate the mind, facilitate movement, and display key information (e.g. key word boxes); how groups and seating are organised to support peer coaching; how to create access to the learning aims for those who struggle with words...

  Differentiation is actually an alternative term for outstanding teaching, learning and assessment. Nearly everything an outstanding teacher does in planning and delivering a unit of work involves interventions to meet the needs of individuals. Leaders need to bear this in mind, therefore, when they ask teachers to complete lesson-planning forms that have a small box called 'differentiation'.

  It is too big a concept for a small box like this and the danger of its use is that weaker teachers insert one or two sentences into the box and think their job is done.

- **Hands-up or no hands-up**

  Teachers the world over will debate the issue of who answers questions – '*volunteers*' or '*conscripts*'? Strong views are expressed by some on this subject, but professional educators will make their own decisions and it may be that the answer is 'it depends...' There is no doubt that some learners in some classes get frustrated if they are denied the opportunity of giving the teacher an answer.

  However, there are learners, either because of shyness or mental truancy, who never want to answer questions and are relieved if the 'hands-up brigade' are allowed to dominate questioning sessions. A 'mixed economy' is, of course, an option, and I am sure there are many teachers who use a wide variety of techniques rather than being philosophically rooted to a single strategy. Some of these options are explored in the menu that follows.

F1 Visual access to learning aims

Some learners with weak literacy skills are helped if teachers display a visual map with words and images showing the 'big picture' of the new topic. It can be printed out for learners.

This technique is also explored in the Purpose of the Lesson section (B9). The example below on healthy living in MfL can be inserted into learners' books or folders and can be annotated with examples either in class or as a homework activity. The map can also serve as a revision map or planning map for writing or speaking. (This visual planning software is available from www.robertpowelltraining.co.uk.)

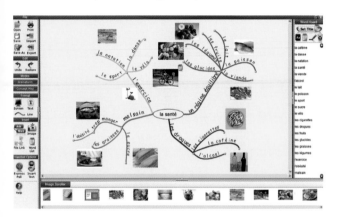

F2 Access to vocabulary

Differentiation includes a focus on key vocabulary – reducing anxiety for weaker readers and widening the technical vocabulary of more confident learners. (See Section D for examples.)

F3 Differentiation by task

This technique requires the teacher to plan learning activities that include tasks of varying degrees of challenge.

This is one of the most common forms of differentiation. The questions or tasks are planned to include a range of challenges.

At the simplest level, differentiation by task might be a set of questions that get more challenging as the learners work through them. A variation on this is where the teacher plans core questions or tasks for the majority of learners but prepares extension tasks for those who show 'mastery' and need challenge, and 'revision' tasks for those who are likely to struggle with the core. More sophisticated versions of this technique are included below.

F4   The Differentiation box

The teacher prepares A5 cards for both challenge and guidance that are stored alphabetically in a card index box like those found in offices or libraries. These are available at any point in a lesson when the teacher identifies a learner needs support or challenge.

Teachers who use this strategy will find all learners asking for a challenge! Challenge or guidance cards can be prepared for any subject or age group – indeed, if teams of teachers plan together in this way, a large stock of them will be available to provide differentiation whenever the need arises. They can be used alongside traditional text books, teacher-prepared tasks or in conjunction with assignments or essays. They can take many forms, from tasks like the ones below to prompts, questions or references, to wider reading or research sites.

In the example below, the teacher has identified learners who are either coasting or struggling on the reading and interpretation of bar graphs. 'Are you finding this easy?' 'Are you finding this hard?' The teacher takes the challenge or guidance card from the storage box and hands it to the learner – 'Have a go at this one then.'

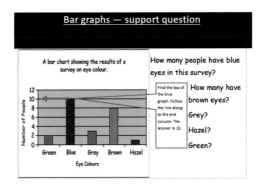

Bar graphs — support question

A bar chart showing the results of a survey on eye colour.

How many people have blue eyes in this survey?

Find the top of the blue graph. Follow the line along to the end column. The answer is 10.

How many have brown eyes? Grey? Hazel? Green?

Number of People (y-axis: 0, 2, 4, 6, 8, 10, 12)

Eye Colours: Green, Blue, Grey, Brown, Hazel

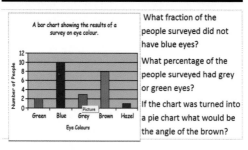

Bar graphs — challenge question

A bar chart showing the results of a survey on eye colour.

What fraction of the people surveyed did not have blue eyes?

What percentage of the people surveyed had grey or green eyes?

If the chart was turned into a pie chart what would be the angle of the brown?

F5 Differentiation over time – planning that uses 'must, should, could'

Teachers planning a unit of work begin by defining differentiated outcomes that will be met by learners over time, recognising that most topics involve a *series* of lessons, not just one.

The lesson plan opposite, which is called a *scheme of learning*, is for a four-lesson unit on endangered animals.

The second column contains the differentiated outcomes using a 'must, should, could' formula. This is not the same as the discredited 'all, most, some' approach still used by some schools. I would urge them to ask themselves if they really want to begin a series of lessons telling a class that only 'some' learners will proceed to the more challenging tasks. So much for aspiration! The key difference, as seen in the example below,

Lesson	Learning outcomes	Phases of lesson	Resources/Support/ homework	Assessment	Skills
1–4	Key question: What animals are endangered, why is this happening and what can be done to protect them? Learners must: ➤ identify which animals are endangered, where they can be found and why they are under threat ➤ list ways that animals can be protected Learners should: ➤ explain why some humans are causing animals to become endangered ➤ identify patterns relating to endangered species Learners could: ➤ evaluate a range of strategies to protect endangered species ➤ produce a manifesto for change	1. Ppt animals (extinct, under threat, fine) decide which. 2. Plot endangered animals around the World. 3. Map with numbers 4. Report from homework the causes of animals being endangered. 5. Categorise (habitat, pollution/climate, commercial, hunting) 6. Jigsaw analysis 7. Revisit map and identify patterns (developing countries) 8. Brainstorm ways to protect animals 9. Produce a visual map of strategies 10. Introduce idea of the manifesto 11. Create the manifesto	Scaffold Animals Ppt Fact sheet and map Map with numbers (extension) Enquiry homework with scaffold Visual map Scaffold Visual map (with images) Scaffold Homework- manifesto poster	Oral feedback Peer assessment Formal	Speaking Whole class and paired work Map skills Paired and small groups Speaking and group collaboration Map skills Formal writing skills

is in the language used; the term 'could' applies to *all* learners. Indeed, in this unit everyone will proceed to the final challenge of creating their own manifesto to save the animals. If teachers use the 'must, should, could' system of differentiation, they must create a set of expectations where all learners aspire to complete the 'could' level of challenge. Note the use of Bloom's verbs in the outcomes.

In this scheme of learning, the third column contains the activities, with a red line showing where the end of that lesson is planned. The fourth column details the resources needed (parallel to the activity) and it is here that teachers might include the role of any teaching assistant. The fifth column details the assessment activity and the final column shows the types of activity or grouping at any point in the four lessons.

The arrow is useful if any visitors enter the classroom to observe. A quick arrow drawn with a red pen shows the visitor where in the four-lesson unit the class is currently working. It shows the new arrival not only what is happening today but what happened in the previous lesson and where the class will proceed in the next. This is far more useful than a single lesson plan, and now that inspectors judge progress 'over time', this format provides a model for lesson planning that supports this process.

Finally, the words in blue signify techniques that are explained in detail in this handbook. A Jigsaw activity involves a complex use of small groups and it would normally require a long explanation in a lesson plan. Here the teacher need only use the key word Jigsaw because the detailed explanation of the activity and its purpose is included in the menu of ideas in the handbook.

A full version of this lesson-planning template, making use of the menus in the handbook/app, appears in the Introduction.

F6   Differentiation through support groups

If small groups are organised with care and the ethos of mutual respect and trust is developed, differentiation can be addressed through peer support.

In Section A on classroom organisation, a cabaret arrangement is shown (A4). If the two pairs who sit opposite each other are chosen carefully, it will be possible to group two students who are relatively confident with two others lacking confidence. If the four students trust each other, the teacher can, on occasions, ask members to support each other. This support can take many forms: clarifying, coaching, modelling and testing for mastery (see F7).

F7   Mastery

The mastery technique involves support groups (F6) revising and practising key knowledge or skills together with the aim of all members of the group achieving mastery.

The mastery technique requires trust within the support group, which allows individuals to ask for or offer guidance from other members. It might, for example, involve the learning of key words in Science. In a mastery activity, the group members of all the support groups practise the meanings of the words together for about 10 minutes. The teacher then sets a test, e.g. 10 questions. The tests are peer-marked instantly and all members of the group combine their marks into a group score, e.g. 36 out of 40. The scores of individuals are not revealed. The only way a group can achieve mastery (40 out of 40) is through peer coaching. This is good for reinforcing the ground rules of trust and empathy: *'in this classroom, if you are not sure, don't worry – someone will help you'*.

F8   'Please help' notice boards

The teacher displays a 'Please help' poster in the classroom. Learners who need help write their names on the board with details of the problem they face. Other learners help them.

The 'Please help' technique also requires an atmosphere of trust in the classroom. This technique is particularly useful in large classes where learners are working independently and sometimes have to wait for a long period for help from the teacher who is circulating the room. In ICT, for example, if a learner writes 'Rob – I don't know how to rotate text' on the 'Please help' board, one of the other learners who knows how to do this will cross out the request on the board and show Rob how to do it.

F9   Focus and Jigsaw groups (A7 and A8)

In this technique the teacher has prepared a range of tasks with varying degrees of challenge. Each member of each group is allocated responsibility for one task.

Focus and Jigsaw groups (see A7 and A8 for more details) are excellent for differentiation. The key is for the teacher to organise the groups carefully to reflect the range of skill or confidence in the class, and then to plan differentiated tasks. The most confident in each of the groups will be allocated the most challenging task, with the least confident members allocated a more accessible task. This should not be seen as a 'fixed' grouping; learners who show great effort and good achievement can be allocated increasingly challenging roles each time this technique is used. With some classes, the teacher may allow the groups to allocate roles – being alert, however, to the dangers of inappropriate choices.

F10   Differentiation through dialogue

Dialogue between learners, their teachers, teaching assistants and peers is a powerful differentiation technique, particularly during periods of independent and small group activity.

Experienced teachers know that often the best way to support or challenge learners is through a one-to-one or small group dialogue. Many learners, reluctant to voice concerns in a whole-class situation, will respond more willingly when they are in a small, trustworthy group or alone with the teacher or teaching assistant. In this more private environment, the teacher can offer personal support or challenge through modelling, skilled questioning or demonstration.

For this to be possible, many of the conditions explored elsewhere in this handbook need to be in place: good classroom management, an ethos of trust, thoughtfully planned groups and differentiated tasks. Differentiation through dialogue involving teachers, teaching assistants and peers is often enhanced if the success criteria for the task are accessible. In the example below, the learners are investigating animals that are endangered and the scaffold (see also F11 below) produced by the teacher includes simple criteria that have been placed at the bottom of the page.

Homework: Endangered species

Animal	What threat?	Evidence	Why threatened?	Who threatens?	What can be done?
Tiger	Hunted Fur and teeth valuable	5,000 tigers left in the World	Fact	Poachers and public buying valuable goods (fur)	Game wardens Stricter laws Ban on sale

Level 3	Level 4	Level 5
List 3 animals under threat	List 3 different types of animal under threat	List 3 animals from different parts of the World
Describe in basic detail why threatened	Identify a number of reasons why each of them is threatened and by whom	Analyse patterns in why animals are threatened
Come up with one idea for protecting them	Identify a number of strategies for protecting animals and select the best two	Evaluate different strategies for protecting animals for their effectiveness

Dialogue about a learner's work can now focus on some of the criteria set out for the investigation. For example:

'You have chosen the Water Vole, the Harris Hawk and the Red Squirrel. That's good, but what does it say for Level 5?'

'List 3 animals from different parts of the world.'

'Why don't you change your list to include animals not found in the UK?'

A scrutiny of learners' exercise books or folders will usually reveal an absence of success criteria. If teachers have a policy of including criteria when learners are planning writing, speaking, designing or making assignments, it will open the door to dialogue like the one above, and this can be done by peer partners as well as teachers or teaching assistants.

Teaching assistants, who are not necessarily specialists in the subject being studied, are helped enormously by the presence of success criteria as are parents and carers if they want to offer support or challenge with their children's homework tasks. When criteria are present, they also provide opportunities for peer-assessment activities (see Section G).

F11 Differentiation through the use of scaffolds

Scaffolds of all types, from the highly structured to the open-ended, can be used to offer support or challenge to learners at all levels in most learning activities.

The term 'scaffold' in education covers a wide range of strategies and techniques that cannot adequately be summarised in a short handbook like this. All scaffolds, however, are designed to provide a structure that will help learners to reach their goals. Scaffolds can be provided through writing, speaking, demonstrating or drama and can be used to help learners structure both content and methods. For example, the scaffold shown in F10 above is a written, grid-type scaffold that supports learners by providing not only the key questions across the top but a modelled example (the tiger) to help them see what is required.

Some scaffolds will provide learners with prompts in the form of questions (possibly using Bloom's taxonomy) or headings. Some may be sentence or paragraph starters and others will be presented orally, e.g. in modern foreign languages. Scaffolds can also be presented visually, as in the map below.

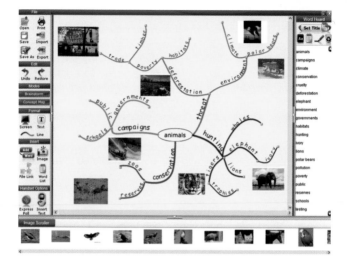

Many learners are anxious when they are asked to plan writing or speaking – they don't know how to start. In this visual scaffold, the topic title is in the middle and there are four main branches or chapters: (1) threats, (2) hunting, (3) conservation and (4) campaigns. The 'twigs' on each branch represent the paragraphs in each chapter. Once learners have this structure, they are able to plan their work more effectively.

The differentiation is also addressed with some branches (e.g. deforestation, poverty and trade) providing conceptual challenges that will extend more confident learners. Other visual forms of scaffolding include story boards where learners write a commentary next to images or photographs, timelines, Venn diagrams, pictorial playing cards, cartoons and, with younger learners, building blocks decorated with words or images.

F12   Differentiation through product

This technique provides learners with the opportunity to demonstrate their understanding or skills in a format of their choice. The teacher might offer them a range of media. Differentiation through product is well used by teachers of creative subjects such as Art, Music, Design, Dance and Drama where the same theme can be interpreted in a wide range of ways and learners make use of a variety of media. The 'product' can vary in other subjects too. If learners were asked, for example, to demonstrate their understanding of why high levels of cholesterol in the blood are potentially unhealthy, the choice of product might include a letter from the health consultant to the patient, the script of a telephone conversation between the doctor and patient, an editorial in a health magazine or a poster for display in a health centre. The scaffold (see F11 above) that would allow this choice would set out the 'ingredients' – key issues and words – that must be addressed in whatever product is chosen. The ingredients can also be differentiated to reduce or increase the level of challenge.

F13   Differentiation through navigation

This technique makes use of existing text books or assignment/question sheets by allowing learners to 'navigate' through the tasks or questions using different routes.

The authors of most text books design them so that when users reach the 'activities' section, the early tasks are relatively easy with the later ones more challenging. A really useful differentiation technique is to offer learners different routes through the questions, depending upon their previous performance or prior learning. A simple instruction 'If you got full marks on yesterday's test, start at Question 10' is quick to implement and prevents some learners from wasting time on tasks that add no value. Some schools extend this concept to homework where a range of homework tasks is published with learners encouraged to select the topic or level that will enable them to spend profitable time at home.

F14   Self-paced, electronic navigation

This differentiation technique allows learners to work through a set of tasks at their own pace using an electronic response system that allows users to 'navigate' the questions.

The *ActivExpression* response handset is not confined to use in schools or colleges with Promethean whiteboards. The response system has a wide range of applications that provide differentiated learning. First, teachers can create a range of differentiated questions with up to eight levels of difficulty.

Questions are sent to the handset screen and learners work at their own pace answering them while teachers monitor the progress of each learner on their laptops or IPads. If teachers choose, they can build in 'live' feedback to learners (see Section G for an example). The handset has a navigation option (see below) that enables teachers to direct learners to different starting points as in F13 above.

One of the most useful aspects of this technology is how it engages the learners and enables them to work independently in silence, freeing up time for teachers to have small group tutorials while everyone else is totally absorbed in their self-paced tasks. Readers who would like to know more about this technology can receive, on request, a free copy of Robert Powell's book *The Response Revolution*, which contains a teacher's guide to its functions. It also has a series of 24 case studies of real lessons submitted by teachers for a range of subjects and age groups from 3-year-olds to post-16 and adult education. Email info@robertpowelltraining.co.uk for your free copy.

F15   Differentiation through ICT

A wide range of ICT hardware and software can be utilised to provide support or challenge to learners.

ActivExpression is not the only technology that supports differentiated learning. The technology available in education is vast and cannot be reviewed in a handbook like this. But teachers will be aware of some key points that are worth considering when planning lessons. Most technology motivates learners. Much of it will allow learners to work at their own pace, on their own products and in a medium of their choice. Technology can be used independently, as part of a group collaboration or as a mass audience activity. What teachers choose to use will depend upon what is available, what school or college policies allow and what is affordable. What is not in doubt is the powerful contribution it can make to the pursuit of differentiated teaching, learning and assessment.

F16   Differentiation through targets and feedback

This technique involves teachers providing written and oral feedback to individuals, which enables them to make progress from their various starting points.

When used effectively, this is one of the purest forms of differentiation. Feedback is a powerful strategy because it can be tailored to the exact needs of the individual. For example, in a class of younger learners the teacher might ask one learner to write on the line, another to use capital letters and full stops, another to start using connectives, another to use more interesting adjectives and yet another to try using a figure of speech such as a metaphor. This type of target is characterised by its immediacy, particularly through oral feedback when learners are working independently, and should be distinguished from longer-term targets where learners are asked to improve performance over time.

One of the benefits of the short-term target is that it can quickly be met by learners and then celebrated by the teacher or teaching assistant. This process can happen several times in a single lesson and can have a huge impact upon the motivation and self-esteem of individuals who can become addicted to this type of success. This technique will be explored in more detail in the next section (G) on assessment and feedback.

Lesson Planning: the menu

Assessment for Learning

Alternative headings

Feedback

Meeting the needs of individuals

See also Section E on Questioning which includes AfL techniques for checking understanding.

Key issues

- **Assessment *of* learning v Assessment *for* learning**

  Data has become increasingly important in schools and colleges, with the measurement of 'progress' often at the heart of judgements made by both leaders and inspection teams. Most schools and college leaders ask teams to provide progress data at regular intervals and this is used to identify issues including perceived under-achievement. The prime purpose of such data is to *inform*, not only leadership, teaching teams, individual teachers, learners and parents but also governments, inspectors and local administration bodies. So while data is incredibly important, it will not be the focus for this section of the handbook and the reason why can be summed up in the well-known phrase *'weighing pigs don't fatten them'*.

  The only way attainment data can be improved is through improving the quality of teaching, learning and assessment. It is formative assessment – featuring regular, targeted and differentiated feedback that delivers progress in attainment, not testing and summative data. Teachers need to use data to *inform* the planning of lessons – a detailed understanding of the prior learning and needs of individuals is essential. This knowledge will allow the teacher to plan differentiation strategies to meet those needs, and the major assessment activity *during* and *between* lessons will be timely feedback to drive lesson-by-lesson progress and to inform subsequent planning.

- **Preparing the ground**

  If teachers are to make the best use of AfL strategies during lessons, they need to have prepared the ground:

  - As John Hattie points out, feedback is only effective if learners want to receive it. Motivated classes are essential as described in Section C on engaging learners.

- If teachers are to be able to offer oral feedback with individuals, learners must be used to working independently. If they are to make the best use of peer-assessment strategies then learners must be used to working collaboratively in groups. So some of the strategies described in Section A on classroom organisation are important to AfL.

- Feedback to the teacher will be enhanced if the strategies described in Section E on Questioning have been addressed.

- Feedback must add challenge so some of the strategies described in Section F on differentiation must be in place.

- **Response to marking (DIRT)**

  The purpose of this handbook is to support teachers in the planning of lessons and so the issue of marking learners' work would not normally feature. However, in recent times the focus on 'progress over time' has encouraged leadership teams to evaluate the impact of marking and feedback on learners' work. Inspection teams now spend time undertaking work scrutiny in order to see if there is evidence of progress and that scrutiny includes judgements on whether the feedback given by teachers has resulted in learning.

  Many schools and colleges have adopted a policy with the acronym DIRT (Dedicated Improvement and Reflection Time) where learners are given time in class in order to improve or edit their work based upon the guidance from teachers, teaching assistants or peers. This strategy now becomes part of lesson planning and will be included in the menu that follows.

- **DIRT and teachers' workload**

  A word of caution on the DIRT policy is necessary. In some schools the implementation of the policy has resulted in an increased workload for teachers who, having marked the work once, are expected to re-mark after the learners have improved it. This workload demand can be alleviated if the policy allows teams to decide how often a DIRT activity takes place and to prioritise some work for the process, not all. Others have chosen not to re-mark but to use a learner response system where learners indicate with a coloured pen or make notes in a learner log when they have acted upon the feedback.

An alternative to DIRT, which appears in the menu below, is Feedforward. With this technique, DIRT becomes redundant if the target can be transferred to the next piece of work, reducing the need for re-marking and in so doing saving a good deal of teaching time.

G1   The criteria for success are clear to all

Hattie called it *Visible Learning*. The teacher has ensured that not only are the success criteria clear to learners and teaching assistants but they are modelled where necessary.

Most teachers share the success criteria with learners, but not all successfully. Many schools and colleges adopt a policy that at the beginning of lessons all teachers should display the '*Objectives, Outcomes and Success criteria*' as in the example below.

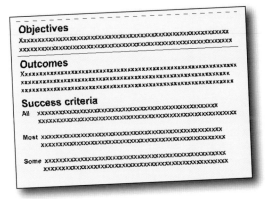

Sharing objectives, outcomes and success criteria is intended to provide clarity of purpose to learners from the beginning of lessons. The formulaic policy above can result in the opposite of what is intended – confusion and anxiety rather than clarity and confidence. Section B on the purpose of the lesson examines this issue in detail, but there are three key reasons why this policy needs to be addressed. First, to the weaker reader the example shown is a mass of words. The terms 'objectives' and 'outcomes' are teacher words and the paragraphs probably contain technical vocabulary or conceptual language that is new and confusing to the learners. Faced with impenetrable language, a number of students will become anxious and simply turn off.

Second, the success criteria for many lessons will refer to a task or assignment that will follow later in the course – it is out of context here and too early to be effective. Third, in the example shown, the teacher is using a differentiation technique of 'all, most, some' that clearly lacks aspiration. The words 'some will' in the English language imply that 'most won't'. Do teachers really want to begin lessons by implying that most learners won't attempt the more challenging aspects of this task? It would be a self-fulfilling prophecy and most won't even try. If teacher expectation is low, so will be learner aspiration.

If the topic only lasts a single lesson then of course the success criteria need to be shared and explained at the beginning. Most topics, however, last more than one lesson, and if an assessed task is to be introduced in lesson 2 or 3 then it would be ineffective to introduce the criteria in lesson 1. It is more effective if success criteria are contextualised – they should be introduced at the point when learners are about to start an assessed task or assignment. A range of alternative techniques for sharing the purpose of learning at the beginning of a topic are described in Section B.

G2 'I can do that' – success criteria are modelled

In this technique, teachers provide examples or 'models' of the success criteria in action, enabling learners to understand what would otherwise be complex and confusing language.

Modelling is one of the most useful techniques for gaining the understanding and confidence of learners about to undertake an assignment. In the example below, the teacher has modelled a Design and Technology design plan to achieve a 'distinction'.

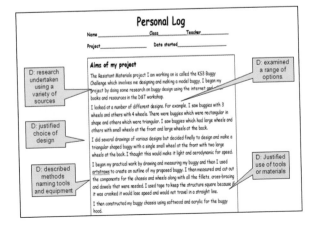

The learners are about to design and make a bird table, so the teacher shows an example of a design plan for an electronic buggy, annotating the parts which awarded it a 'distinction'. Learners will have to transfer their understanding of this to their bird table assignment.

Modelling can take a number of forms. Teachers can model work with the whole class, editing and improving a test answer on the whiteboard with contributions from learners. Teachers of practical subjects will often use other learners to model activity – e.g. in Music, PE, Art and Dance. Most teachers of Science or vocational subjects in colleges will model practical activity with machinery or equipment before students are asked to use it. Teachers of modern foreign languages will model spoken language and early years' learners have always learnt by watching their older peers demonstrating a skill. The aim, of course, of all these different styles of modelling is for learners to be able to say 'I can do that'.

G3   DIRT (Directed Improvement and Reflection Time)

The teacher's oral or written feedback to learners indicates one or more targets for improvement and time is allocated in class or homework for them to enact the guidance.

This technique, discussed in key issues above, is designed to ensure that the targets provided to learners in feedback are acted upon, demonstrating progress. There is a wide variety of DIRT systems in use in schools, most of them involving the use of coloured pens. For example, if a teacher's feedback indicates that learners must 'write in sentences' then in a DIRT activity they redo the work in sentences in a purple pen. Teachers either check that this has been done or learners keep a progress log where they record their response to the feedback.

In some schools where exercise books are used, drafts of learners' work are on the left-hand side of the book. Teachers, teaching assistants and peers offer feedback that is recorded in the margin with words, codes or coloured dots (e.g. a red dot or cross may indicate spelling or grammar – see G4 below), the learners take the advice and the resulting 'best work' is written on the right-hand side. This technique can be central to a marking policy where only the work on the right-hand side is formally marked, with the drafts on the left subject to oral feedback from teachers, teaching assistants or peers. An alternative to DIRT is described below in Feedforward (G8).

G4 Assessment codes for feedback or targets

A quick and easy way to provide live feedback is to publish targets in the form of coded 'can do' statements, enabling teachers, TAs or peers to set targets using a simple code.

In the two examples below, one for literacy and one for numeracy, the 'personal logs' have been displayed as posters and the learners all have them in their books, folders or planners. Targets from the logs can be agreed in a number of ways: the learner chooses a target, the teacher or TA suggests a target or a peer can set the target.

A1 I use I, not i	A2 I use a full stop at the end of a sentence.	A3 I can use a comma.	A4 I can use a capital letter at the beginning of a sentence.	A5 I can use a capital letter for proper names.
A6 I can use a question mark.	A7 I can write in sentences.	A8 I write on the lines.	A9 I start sentences with different words.	A10 I use my ruler.
A11 I can use connecting words.	A12 I can do joined-up writing.	A13 I put my date and heading at the top.	A14 I can keep my writing straight.	A15 I can keep my letters the same size.
A16 I bring a pen, pencil, ruler and rubber to school.	A17 I help others when they are stuck.	A18 I am a good listener.	A19 I start work straight away when asked.	A20 I put my work away at the end of a lesson.

A1 I can add 3-digit whole numbers together.	A2 I can add whole numbers of any size.	A3 I can add decimals with 2 decimal places.	A4 I can add decimals with 3 decimal places.	A5 I can add whole numbers and decimals in everyday contexts.
A6 I can subtract 3-digit whole numbers.	A7 I can subtract whole numbers of any size.	A8 I can subtract decimals with 2 decimal places.	A9 I can subtract decimals with 3 decimal places.	A10 I can subtract whole numbers and decimals in everyday contexts.
A11 I can multiply 2-digit whole numbers by a single whole number.	A12 I can multiply 2-digit whole numbers by 2-digit whole numbers.	A13 I can multiply a decimal by a whole number up to 2 decimal places.	A14 I can multiply a decimal by a decimal.	A15 I can multiply whole numbers and decimals in everyday contexts.
A16 I can divide a 2-digit number by a single whole number.	A17 I can divide a 3-digit number by a single digit whole number and interpret remainders.	A18 I can divide a decimal by a single digit whole number and interpret remainders.	A19 I can divide a decimal by a decimal.	A20 I can divide whole numbers and decimals in everyday contexts.

If such a log is kept in the learners' books or planners, they can be awarded a 'smiley face' or 'target achieved' stamp once they have consistently demonstrated the skill.

A1 😊 I use I, not i	A2 😊 I use a full stop at the end of a sentence.	A3 😊 I can use a comma.	A4 😊 I can use a capital letter at the beginning of a sentence.	A5 I can use a capital letter for proper names.
A6 I can use a question mark.	A7 😊 I can write in sentences.	A8 😊 I write on the lines.	A9 I start sentences with different words.	A10 😊 I use my ruler.
A11 I can use connecting words.	A12 I can do joined-up writing.	A13 I put my date and heading at the top.	A14 😊 I can keep my writing straight.	A15 I can keep my letters the same size.
A16 I bring a pen, pencil, ruler and rubber to school.	A17 I help others when they are stuck.	A18 😊 I am a good listener.	A19 I start work straight away when asked.	A20 I put my work away at the end of a lesson.

A1 I can add 3-digit whole numbers together. 🎯	A2 I can add whole numbers of any size. 🎯	A3 I can add decimals with 2 decimal places.	A4 I can add decimals with 3 decimal places. 🎯	A5 I can add whole numbers and decimals in everyday contexts.
A6 I can subtract 3-digit whole numbers. 🎯	A7 I can subtract whole numbers of any size. 🎯	A8 I can subtract decimals with 2 decimal places.	A9 I can subtract decimals with 3 decimal places.	A10 I can subtract whole numbers and decimals in everyday contexts.
A11 I can multiply 2-digit whole numbers by a single whole number.	A12 I can multiply 2-digit whole numbers by 2-digit whole numbers.	A13 I can multiply a decimal by a whole number up to 2 decimal places.	A14 I can multiply a decimal by a decimal.	A15 I can multiply whole numbers and decimals in everyday contexts.
A16 I can divide a 2-digit number by a single whole number. 🎯	A17 I can divide a 3-digit number by a single digit whole number and interpret remainders.	A18 I can divide a decimal by a single digit whole number and interpret remainders.	A19 I can divide a decimal by a decimal.	A20 I can divide whole numbers and decimals in everyday contexts.

When the learners have mastered all the skills in the log, they are moved onto a more challenging version.

Many schools and colleges already use punctuation codes and the technique above is simply extending this practice. It is possible, of course, for teachers of any age or subject to use codes both for oral feedback in class (see G5 below) and for marking work at home. If you mark assignments at home and have a large class of 25–30 learners, imagine how long it takes to write *'next time please use some evidence from the text to support your conclusions'* and other such comments in the margins of 25 essays. Such feedback can be replaced by codes, e.g. *'C7'*, provided all learners know exactly what C7 means. The saving in teacher marking time is enormous.

Another reason why a published set of skills codes is useful is because it defines for learners what constitutes good practice. This is not only important for defining academic or vocational skills but also for defining expectations with regard to classroom behaviour. A set of codes like the ones below, displayed in classrooms, makes it absolutely clear what 'good behaviour' looks like.

B1 I arrive on time.	B2 I go straight to my place and sit down.	B3 I put my hand up when I want to speak.	B4 I listen to instructions.	B5 I sit where I am told to sit.
B6 I can sit quietly for 5 minutes or more.	B7 I do not wander around.	B8 I do not stop others working.	B9 I show respect to others.	B10 I follow classroom rules.
B11 I admit it when I am in the wrong.	B12 I say sorry when I am wrong.	B13 I do not make fun of others.	B14 I thank others when they help me.	B15 I keep my temper.
B16 I do not shout in school.	B17 I look after my books and equipment.	B18 I never throw things.	B19 I do not draw or write graffiti on my books.	B20 I put away my books and equipment.

G5 Oral feedback

Oral feedback can often be more effective than written comments. It works for all ages and subjects, particularly practical ones. This technique ensures oral feedback leads to learning.

There is no doubt that oral feedback from skilled teachers or teaching assistants is highly effective in the process of supporting or challenging learners, particularly when it involves a dialogue and, on occasions, the modelling of practice. If teachers are to find time for effective dialogue then learners need to have the ability to work independently or in groups. Some of the strategies explored in Section A on classroom organisation will help with the time issues, and techniques such as scaffolding described in Section F on differentiation will also enable learners to work independently.

The most challenging issue with oral feedback, however, is ensuring that the guidance is not forgotten – many teachers of all subjects and phases will have experienced learners who nod in agreement during the discussion and then promptly forget to enact the advice. Now that inspection teams are looking for evidence of how feedback aids progress over time, the pressure on teachers to make oral feedback count is even greater.

One technique that is effective in this regard is the use of coloured pens or ink stamps. In the example below, the teacher has asked the learner to start using paragraphs. The learner uses a green pen immediately to record the memo in the margin (this is where a code might be used – see G4 above). When the learner uses paragraphs and shows the teacher, the smiley face (or achievement stamp) is awarded. It is remarkable how quickly learners respond to feedback when they receive an instant reward.

This process is clear evidence that progress has been made as a result of oral feedback. This system is powerful partly because of its simplicity – no one wants to use bureaucratic systems – and partly because it creates a learner addiction to the rewards; the quicker they enact the guidance, the quicker they get their stickers.

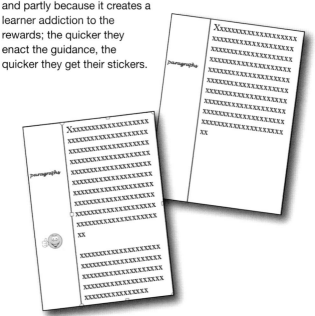

G6 Oral feedback and learning logs using ICT/technology

This technique shows how oral feedback in live classrooms can be recorded by students through the use of electronic learning logs.

There are many courses in schools and colleges where learners work independently or in groups for a large percentage of their contact time with teachers. Teachers of practical or vocational subjects are faced with the challenge of monitoring the progress of often large classes, where learners might even be working on personal assignments that are markedly different from those of their peers. Younger learners in some schools sometimes work on projects and their progress on these needs monitoring. In both situations, most of the feedback will be oral. The need for some kind of personal log is heightened when formal assessment is some way off and it is the formative assessment, lesson to lesson, which is driving and motivating the learners.

When learners have access to ICT, a program like Excel can be used for recording progress and feedback. The illustration below shows how such a system might work.

	A	B	C	D	E	F
1	Name:					
2	Target Grade:					
3	Unit	Lesson Number and Date	Today's Tasks	Evaluation	Feedback (Red to do and Green once completed)	Merit / Sanction
4		1	Insert graphics, add commentary	Completed graphics, started commentary	Need more than one type of graphic	
5		2	Finish commentary, add different type of graphic			
6		3				
7		4				
8		5				
9		6				
10	5 - Desktop	7				
11	Publishing	8				
12		9				
13		10				
14		11				
15		12				
16		13				
17		14				
18		15				
19		16				

Learners are required to maintain these logs. The example is from an ICT course but the same idea will work for any subject where learners work independently on assignments and have access to ICT – Music is a prime example.

Learners record in the *Today's Tasks* column their work plan for each lesson. Towards the end of each lesson, they have to complete their evaluation column on the progress made and then complete the log before they leave their work plan for lesson 2. During the lesson the teacher will have circulated the classroom, questioning, supporting and challenging learners with oral feedback. In the example shown, the teacher's feedback included advice that another type of graphic was needed. The learner made a memo of that immediately in the Feedback column in a red font (or red cell if in Excel). Red indicates that the feedback has not yet been implemented. The learner adds this task to the plan for lesson 2. (This is a form of *feedforward*, examined below in G8.) During the next lesson, the learner adds the new graphic as per the plan and shows the teacher. The teacher approves the work and the target in the Feedback column is changed to a green font or cell colour as in the illustration below.

The green indicates that the feedback has been implemented. This style of personal log will remind learners of what tasks have still to be completed and provides teachers with an easy-to-use monitoring system. The merit/detention column can be used to celebrate excellent progress or to reprimand those who may have been off-task and wasted time. Any visitor to the classroom can ask learners to open their logs and progress 'over time' can be viewed instantly.

If the log was being used for Music, another column could be added for hyperlinks to recordings of a composition at any time. Visitors to music rooms will be able to listen to the various stages of a composition, e.g. after two weeks, four weeks etc. This is an excellent way to demonstrate progress 'over time' in this subject. If ICT is available to learners studying other creative subjects, the same concept will be effective but the final column might contain hyperlinks to photographs or video recordings logging progress of the project.

Such personal logs can also be used by teachers to establish clear purpose at the beginning of lessons. If all learners arrive in the classroom and immediately open their logs, the teacher can ask them to add any targets or reminders to the feedback column.

Some schools and colleges are beginning to use hand-held technology for recording oral feedback. Coleg Cambria in North Wales won an award for their use of mobile phones for logging feedback. The college has developed an app that is used by some vocational teams to good effect. Oral feedback identifying 'steps forward' is logged instantly by learners on their mobile phones as a reminder. As one lecturer remarked, '…students may forget their folders but they never forget their phones'.

G7 Oral feedback and learning logs (non-ICT)

This technique shows how oral feedback in live classrooms can be recorded by students through the use of paper-based personal logs.

A process similar to the one described in G6 above can be adopted by teachers even when there is no learner access in the classroom to ICT. Most teachers of courses where learners have to work independently on assignments for a significant amount of time will have logging systems – similar to the concept of sketch books used by teachers of Art. These will vary in design and will often reflect the demands of examination boards. The addition of two sections or columns, as in the example below, to whatever style of log is used, will enable learners to create a memo from the oral feedback and teachers to monitor the impact by awarding the achievement sticker when the guidance has been enacted. The dates show progress over time.

Date	Feedback	Achieved	Date
10/9	*Remember to:.....*	Target ◎ Achieved!	12/9
12/9	*I need to try and...*	Target ◎ Achieved!	17/9
17/9	*I am going to try to:...*	Target ◎ Achieved!	20/9
20/9	*I must think about how...*		

G8   Feedforward

This technique involves learners moving the *feedback* from the teacher or TA *forward* to the beginning of the new piece of work as a reminder to both learner and teacher.

Feedforward is an alternative approach to DIRT (G3) and in some contexts is a more effective option. Some feedback needs to be acted upon immediately. For example, in a science lesson on electrical circuits, confusion over the difference between a series and a parallel circuit needs to be dealt with as a DIRT activity because the next lesson is on the topic of cells. Similarly, confusion in mathematics over simplifying fractions must be tackled before the teacher switches to a new topic on algebra.

However, it may not be necessary to act on all feedback as a DIRT activity. If the feedback refers to an ongoing skill, learners can feedforward to the next piece of work. Ongoing targets are like those below.

- *Write in full sentences*
- *Show your working*

- *Use a wider range of sources*
- *Remember to put in your accents*
- *Label your diagrams*
- *Use more interesting adjectives and adverbs*

There is no need for learners to act upon such targets as a DIRT activity – this will waste teaching time. It is far more effective if they simply feedforward the target to the next piece of work as in the example below.

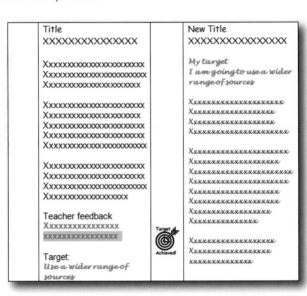

The target is moved from the last piece of work to the top of the new work using the convention 'I am going to...'. This reminds the learner and the teacher. The key to making this work is the reward that the learner receives when they have enacted the guidance. The teacher places a target achieved sticker in the margin once they see the evidence of the learner 'using a wider range of sources'. There are two very important benefits of this feedforward system. First, learners can become addicted to the reward stickers, so will enact their targets immediately and show the teacher. This changes ethos and aspiration. Second, any scrutiny of work to look for evidence of progress over time is easy. Every time a target appears at the top of a page with a sticker below, this is evidence of progress; the learner has improved in line with the feedback previously offered.

The same system can be adopted with the use of skills codes (G4). The teacher may give feedback that identifies A4 and A5 as targets (see chart in G4). At the beginning of the next piece of work, the learner writes:

My target: I am going to:

(1) use a capital letter at the beginning of my sentences

(2) use a capital letter for proper names.

G9 Peer assessment

Peer assessment is used to help learners understand the criteria for success and to provide them with opportunities to improve work and performance after feedback from friends.

Peer assessment is widely used in schools and colleges, but the quality and effectiveness of the practice vary widely. At its worst, learners assess each other's work with little guidance from the teacher and with the sole purpose of saving teacher marking time. Fortunately such practice is rare, and the majority of practitioners recognise the value peer assessment can add when introduced within a set of clear guidelines.

First, the key purpose of peer assessment must be to train learners in the art of assessment; if they can recognise the features of an outstanding performance or piece of work then they are better placed to plan their own. The phrase '*getting learners inside the head of examiners*' is a useful description of the process. Second, if this process is to be effective, learners must be trained to become 'assessors'. Success criteria must be shared and modelled (refer to G1 and G2 above) and practice sessions organised to equip learners with the skills needed. Third, teachers must agree guidelines for when peer assessment will be used. For example, many teachers will not use it if the work to be assessed is a topic new to the class.

One of the prime purposes of marking is to provide feedback to the teacher, so with new topics it is essential that the teacher assesses the work in order to see if the skills or knowledge have been mastered. On the other hand, tasks designed to give learners practice in answering examination questions are ideal for peer assessment provided time has been spent beforehand in modelling answers. Once these guidelines have been implemented, the techniques below can be added to teachers' repertoire of peer-assessment activities.

G10   Peer-assess a stranger's work

This is a training activity for peer assessment where learners assess the work of a student they do not know – e.g. an assignment from a previous year or one produced by the teacher.

Teachers should prepare the learners by sharing the success criteria for the task and modelling as a class activity. The assignment selected for the peer-assessment activity should have all the written comments removed before copying (or showing on a screen using a visualiser or a photograph taken with a camera).

Learners should be organised into small groups and provided with a copy of the success criteria. They are then asked to assess the work, awarding it a grade or level if appropriate, noting evidence to support their conclusions. When the assessment is complete, one group comes out to the front and reveals the grade awarded. Other groups are asked to speak if they disagree and the lesson proceeds as groups defend their position by pointing to the evidence they have produced to support their arguments. This is a useful starting point for training in peer assessment because there is no emotional connection to the person being assessed – it is not their friend but the work of a stranger.

G11   Peer-assess a presentation

In this activity, small groups need to prepare a presentation. Beforehand the whole class agrees the success criteria to be used. Each presentation is then peer-assessed.

This technique can be used to assess any practical activity such as a presentation, a role-play, a demonstration in physical education, a dance routine, a scene in drama or a host of activities in vocational subjects. The purpose is for the learners to improve their understanding and skills in such activities, and to do this they must not only take on the role of presenter but also of evaluator.

Having organised the groups, teachers should begin by explaining the scope and purpose of the presentation. They should then involve the whole class in agreeing the success criteria for a 'good' presentation. Headings such as 'audience', 'content', 'engagement', 'technical skills', 'voice and body language' might be agreed. Each of these should then be expanded to define 'good' practice and then displayed on posters.

Groups then plan their presentations in line with the agreed criteria and when each presentation takes place, the other groups are given roles as evaluators: one group for content, one for technical skills, one for audience and so on. After each presentation the evaluation groups meet and prepare their feedback, possibly using the convention '*what went well*' (WWW) and '*even better if*' (EBI). Learners are engaged throughout and subsequent presentations improve because of the peer-assessment process.

G12   Peers solve the mystery

Teachers mark work with a tick (like), a cross (mistake) and a question mark (something not quite right) in the margin. Peer partners try to solve the mystery of why they are there.

This technique involves peer dialogue but is also useful as a training activity for self-evaluation. Teachers use three coloured pens when marking work, awarding a tick when they like something, a cross when there is a mistake or a question mark when something is not quite right (e.g. grammar, no evidence presented, poor judgement etc.). No explanation is offered by teachers and the work is returned to the learners. Their task, with their peer partners, is to solve the mystery. Why did the teacher like that? What is the mistake in that sentence? What is wrong with that paragraph?

This is good training on assessment because they start to read the minds of their teachers, who in this instance are their 'examiners'. 'Getting inside the head of examiners' is once again reinforced as a process for improving overall performance in assessed work.

G13   Peers find the mistake

The teacher looks at a piece of work, makes no corrections but records at the bottom the number of mistakes seen. Learners in pairs have to find and correct the errors.

This technique works particularly well in lessons on numeracy and literacy. '*There are three mistakes on this page*' (or '*in this paragraph*') is quite a stimulating challenge for learners, who engage in dialogue to find the errors. Once learners find the mistakes, they consult the teacher and if they are right they then do the corrections in whatever colour pen the school policy dictates. This works well in pairs, with the dialogue a form of peer tutoring as they talk through what they think might be mistakes.

G14   Self-reflection

This strategy asks learners to reflect on their own work or performance. This process is designed to help them to move from first ideas to final product, improving at each stage.

Teachers of practical subjects or vocational courses involving 'making and doing' have always placed great emphasis on self-evaluation. The sketch book in Art, for example, is a good example of the process whereby initial ideas are explored, developed, refined or rejected. The same process of self-reflection will be evident in the work of poets, composers and authors, most of whom will confess to being their own greatest critic.

The same process of reflection and improvement can be used in most subjects and with learners of most ages. As with peer assessment, training is the key. Many teachers who use self-reflection to good effect, particularly those who work with younger learners, use success criteria in the form of a check list pasted into the book at the top of the work, as in the simple example below. They tick the box when they have demonstrated the skill. Some check lists have an additional column for peers to comment.

✓	Use capital letters and full stops.
✓	Use interesting connectives.
✓	Use interesting adjectives
✓	Use interesting adverbs
✓	Use a metaphor or simile
✓	Use verbs ending in
✓	Organise into paragr

✓	Use capital letters for proper names
✓	Use a semi colon correctly
✓	Use a colon correctly
✓	Use simple, compound and complex sentences
✓	Use alliteration
✓	Use personification
✓	Use present, future and past tenses

The same concept applied to older learners might involve the use of question boxes as displayed in the example in E12 in the section on questioning. The scaffold on Endangered Animals shown in F10 lists the success criteria at the bottom, providing the means for learners to undertake a self-review of the first draft. There are two key messages for teachers wishing to add self-reflection to their repertoire of assessment techniques. First, the success criteria are vital ingredients of this process and learners must be trained in their use. Second, self-assessment is much harder than peer assessment, so practise peer assessment first.

G15   Electronic feedback for self-reflection

This technique makes use of *ActivExpression* response technology. It sends live feedback to learners, can offer guidance, and provides them with the chance to reflect upon errors.

This technology was described in Section F14 as a powerful tool for differentiation with its self-paced and navigation functions. It is also the best technology currently available for live feedback to learners. All learners have handsets registered in their names. This allows teachers to watch on their screens as learners answer questions.

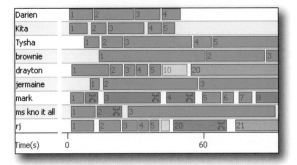

The colour codes the difficulty level of the question, the length of bar shows how long each learner spent on the question and a cross tells the teacher a mistake has been made. The navigation function allows the learner called drayton to go straight to Q10 because he found the first five too easy.

When teachers see a cross, they can hover over that question and it shows what the learner has answered. Mark has misunderstood his percentages. The teacher has 'live' feedback of a problem and can intervene immediately.

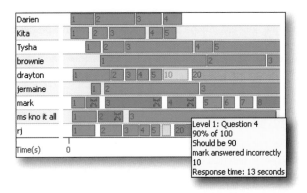

This 'live' feedback to the teacher means that guidance can be offered at the time the learner needs it – if this task was being done in exercise books, the teacher would have been fortunate to spot the mistake in a large group while circulating, and if it is spotted when marking the books, it will be too late to influence the learning.

The technology can also offer feedback to the learners. In the example below, the teacher has anticipated the BIDMAS rule being forgotten and has added guidance when preparing the questions.

The learner does the calculation and answers '30'. Instantly, a message appears on the learner's screen with a reminder of the BIDMAS rule. Without such guidance, the learner would have made the same mistake with the next three questions.

This process is termed 'Questions for learning' – the activity is not about measuring, but learning. When a mistake is made, feedback is offered, a correct answer follows and learning has taken place.

The same process can work with basic literacy skills.

The most effective feedback is when learners have just made a mistake and this technology does exactly that. The analysis function saves on hours of marking and the results of assessments can be used in the planning of future lessons.

The final function of the technology that is relevant to this section of the menu is the way it can be used to encourage self-reflection. In the example below, I observed a teacher of mathematics teach a group of 13-year-olds about graphing quadratic functions. To test their understanding, she placed a large poster on the classroom wall with a number of different graphs labelled A to N – two of them are reproduced below.

H1   Merit system

A system of merits is used by many schools. The criteria will vary but merits can be awarded for achievement, progress or effort and can link to Form, Year or House competitions.

This is the most common system of rewards or celebration, used primarily in schools with younger learners. In a few schools they are actually linked to financial rewards but most are used as a boost to self-esteem and linked to progress on defined targets. This system of celebration is most successful when all teachers and teaching assistants actively participate.

H2   Stickers or stamps

This technique involves teachers or teaching assistants (and sometimes peers) awarding an achievement sticker or stamp to reward and celebrate when a short-term target is met.

Examples of this in practice appear in the section on Assessment for Learning (G4, G5, G6, G7 and G8).

H3   Celebration noticeboard

This technique involves the teacher having a noticeboard in the classroom or corridor to display work that the teacher, teaching assistants or peers deem worthy of celebration.

This noticeboard is different from those normally used to display work because this display is celebrating outstanding work or performance. This does not mean that only the work of the most skilled or talented learners is on display – if 'ipsative' assessment is used then a 'personal best' is enough to qualify – it is 'outstanding' in relation to that learner's previous efforts.

H4   Celebration timeline

This technique works well with smaller classes. A timeline is displayed month by month on the wall and learners select a piece of work to be displayed as 'work of the month'.

I worked with a comprehensive in Essex that had its own centre for learners with special needs. A timeline was on the wall, starting with September and going around the wall as far as July. Beneath each date, learners had placed an example of 'my best work'. One learner showed me her work from September and when I praised it she said *'No, it's rubbish!'* and taking me by the hand she walked around to January. *'Look at my work now'* she proudly boasted; celebration at its best.

H5   Celebration folder

This technique is like H4 above, but instead of displaying best work each month on a wall display, learners place their chosen work in a plastic wallet inside a mock-leather folder.

These mock-leather folders, available in most stationers, contain 20 or more plastic wallets. The learners, after discussion with their teachers or teaching assistants, select pieces of work from each month that they think is their 'best'. A date is added to the top of the page. This becomes a personal record for each learner of the progress made over a year. Some learners, particularly those with special needs, believe that progress is impossible and this monthly record, which shows real development over time, is a wonderful record and can do much to raise the aspiration and confidence of those who find learning difficult.

The folder can be viewed at parents' consultation sessions and can be transferred between year groups and even schools as the learners get older.

H6   Celebration certificate

This technique involves using certificates of achievement when learners reach a milestone in their learning. This works well when used in conjunction with skills logs (G4).

The logs shown in G4 can have a huge impact upon motivation. Learners are desperate to have smiley faces for all 20 skills and then move on to the higher-level log. This motivation can be enhanced if the completion of the log is followed by a certificate ceremony, which can range from a quiet and private word from the teacher to a proper ceremony in an assembly. If behaviour logs, as in the example in G4, are primarily used to identify those learners who are causing concerns, then the well-behaved learners may feel aggrieved. There is no reason why an electronic system of the behaviour log can not only identify miscreants, but also those with a perfect behaviour record who receive a certificate as recognition.

H7   Celebration ladder

A ladder with a number of steps is placed in all learners' exercise books related to a key skill, e.g. literacy. When learners achieve a target, their cartoon character climbs a step.

This technique works well with younger learners. The cartoon character celebrates by moving up the ladder as skills are mastered. The visual nature of this type of reward can be extended to other methods of climbing – trees, mountains, space.

H8   Celebration fanfare

A fanfare (cheers, applause, trumpets/brass) is installed on the computer, whiteboard or tablet. When learners say something worthy of celebration, the teacher plays the fanfare.

This works really well for celebrating oral work. Whether it is a point made really well in a discussion, speaking in the foreign language with great skill, using a key technical term from a word box on the wall, asking a good question or answering one with great lucidity, oral work can be celebrated with this simple device.

H9   Headteacher award

This technique involves sending learners who have achieved personal bests to see the Headteacher or Principal. They are congratulated and sent back with an award/sticker.

I used this technique when I was a headteacher. Teachers would send any student who achieved a personal best to my office and, unless I was in a confidential meeting, I would always find time to see them. I would receive students with written work, art

work or design models, students
with cakes and sometimes a trio
from music who would sing to
me. They all left my office with
a sticker like the one shown
(*thanks to School Merit
Stickers*) – Year 7s with it
proudly on their chests and Year
11s with it hidden under their
jackets!

On one occasion a whole class of students arrived with history
assignments that had all been graded A. The 40 minutes it took
me to look at all the work and award the stickers was well
spent.

H10   Celebration media

Many schools and colleges now have TV screens around their
buildings. During a set time each day, perhaps break times,
learners' achievements are celebrated on news screens.

This system needs an editorial team to put together the daily
celebration news but there will be no shortage of volunteers for
such an exciting venture. Teachers, teaching assistants,
community groups, governors and local businesses can all
nominate learners to appear on the 'news' show and the
celebration could relate to any kind of success – great progress,
academic excellence, social responsibility, work in the
community, sporting success, artistic merit, musical
accomplishment, engineering designs, wonderful performance
in drama or dance – the list is endless.

Creating a culture of learning that values more than just
academic success is a characteristic of great schools and
colleges, and this initiative will cement all other forms of
classroom celebration, including those described above.

How to use the menus to save teachers time and to enrich teaching, learning and assessment

The menus in the preceding chapters or menus produced in-house by teams of teachers are now ready. This chapter now examines how they might be used (a) to save teachers hours of planning time and (b) to widen the use of the best techniques and strategies identified through the collaboration of staff.

How to use the menu

Each technique or idea in the menus contained a code, e.g. '**A8**', and a key word or phrase, e.g. '**Jigsaw (or Envoy)**'. After each key word there was a short explanation or example for illustration purposes. If a teacher decides to share the overall purpose of the learning with a class by displaying a visual map, the lesson plan will show under its learning aims heading the phrase '**B9. Visual map or overview**'. No further detail is required on a lesson-plan form – the explanation for an observer is in the handbook (just look up **B9**) and the lesson aims flipchart is on display in the classroom. Teachers need to spend their time *planning* resources like a visual map or a key words box, not writing an explanation on a form.

The app version of the menu allows users to import whatever lesson-planning form they are required to use – even if it is a proverbial 'back of an envelope'. They can add their own techniques to the ones already on the app and then simply scroll down and select which ideas or techniques to use. They import them onto their planning form and edit them in whatever way they choose. The menu approach is designed to enrich classroom techniques and also to save teachers hours of planning time. The example below of the planning of a lesson on Victorian life will illustrate both points.

Example 1: Victorian life: outline of lesson plan

- The lesson begins with the teacher showing a PowerPoint with music displaying 20 photographs that give learners clues about the Victorian era. Images include a classroom with slates for writing on, factories with child labour, a workhouse, slum buildings, malnourished children, police officers, child prisoners and wealthy people with carriages. Victorian music plays as the images scroll through.

- The learners are given five minutes in their support groups to come up with questions about the photographs. The questions are turned skilfully by the teacher into lesson objectives with a series of 'You will be able to answer the following questions…' These are then displayed on the wall.

- Having engaged the learners, the teacher introduces the research activity that is to follow on four aspects of Victorian life: (a) child labour, (b) living conditions for the poor, (c) the workhouse and (d) crime.

- Each member of the cabaret groups is allocated one of the four focus areas. The more confident readers are advised to focus on area a or area b and the others to focus on area c or area d. The learners move into their Jigsaw groups.

- Each focus group is provided with a scaffold to aid the research. The scaffolds are differentiated using Bloom's taxonomy – scaffolds a and b include more challenging questions than scaffolds c and d.

- In conducting their research, learners must make use of the key word poster (with scores) and start to use the correct terminology from the era. Each learner in each group must compile a fact sheet based on the scaffolds' questions and prompts.

- The jigsaw ends with each Jigsaw group member returning to their original cabaret group where they take it in turns to teach the others all they have learned about Victorian life in relation to the focus each studied.

- The teacher then introduces the writing task, sharing the success criteria and modelling aspects before the task begins. All learners paste the success criteria into their exercise books. Learners choose their product (a diary of a pickpocket, an interview with a charity worker about living conditions, a newspaper editorial about child labour or a 'day in the life' of a person from the workhouse).

- Learners are asked to set out personal literacy targets from their skills' logs at the top of the page.

  During the writing activity, feedback is given orally by TAs and the teacher and recorded by learners using green pens. Smiley-face stickers are used when learners act upon the feedback.

- Final drafts are peer-checked against the success criteria before final products are completed and then assessed formally by the teacher.

Using the handbook or app menu, the same lesson can be planned very quickly 'on the back of an envelope' as in the example below.

'Back of the envelope' planning
This version of the lesson plan sets out the same sequence of activities using codes and key words from the menu. There is no need to provide detailed descriptions of activities such as the Jigsaw because this is done in the handbook.

This plan is primarily for the teacher who has chosen the activities from the menu and understands what each code or heading means. If an observer needs to know what the codes mean, they can simply consult the handbook. This version of the lesson plan took only a fraction of the time lesson-planning normally takes but still incorporates a wide range of excellent practice.

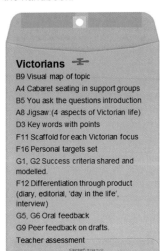

Victorians
B9 Visual map of topic
A4 Cabaret seating in support groups
B5 You ask the questions introduction
A8 Jigsaw:(4 aspects of Victorian life)
D3 Key words with points
F11 Scaffold for each Victorian focus
F16 Personal targets set
G1, G2 Success criteria shared and modelled.
F12 Differentiation through product (diary, editorial, 'day in the life', interview)
G5, G6 Oral feedback
G9 Peer feedback on drafts.
Teacher assessment

This saving in time will now allow the teacher to collect Victorian resources, to prepare the word box and the scaffolds and to design and copy the success criteria for pasting into the learners' exercise books. It is this type of planning that leads to outstanding lessons, not filling in lesson-planning forms. Teacher exhaustion comes when they are required to do both.

Example 2: More detailed lesson-plan format
Where a more detailed lesson format is required by the school or college, the same lesson on Victorian life can be set out quickly by selecting techniques from the menu and importing them to the template. Once again, the detailed description of each activity is unnecessary – they are set out in the handbook or on the app.

The template used in the lesson plan above is just one example of the many forms used by schools and colleges – the layout is immaterial – ideas and techniques can be imported into whatever headings are used. The key is for groups of staff in a year team or a department (or even the whole staff in a small school or groups of teachers from a chain of schools or academies) to agree on the wide range of techniques used and give them a code or heading that everyone understands.

Date: xx xx xx		Lesson: 3 lessons	Year: xxxx	Levels: xxxx	Tutor: xxxxx
Topic: Victorian life					
	Time	Plan			
Starter activity	10 mins	B5 Learners ask the questions. Victorian life PowerPoint with images and music. B9 Visual map.			
Learning objective and outcome	15 mins	You will be able to answer the following questions: 1. What were living conditions like for the poor in Victorian times? 2. Why did children have to work in factories? 3. How and why were children involved in crime? 4. What were workhouses and why did they exist?			
Main Activity 1	1.5 lessons	A8 Jigsaw activity on 4 aspects of Victorian life. Scaffolds provided.			
Homework		Further research on Victorian life based on scaffold questions.			
Extension work	Ongoing	A8. F16. (Personal targets for individuals.)			
Plenary	30 minutes	A4. Return to original cabaret groups. Feedback.			
Main activity 2	1 lesson	Extended F12. (A diary of a pickpocket, an interview with a charity worker about living conditions, a newspaper editorial about child labour or a 'day in the life' of a person from the workhouse.) G9.			
Extra-Curricular		Possible visit to museum if available.			
Assessment AfL	ongoing	F1. G1 and G2. G5 and G6. G9.			
Key Words		D3			
Differentiation		A4. B9. A8. F12. F1.			
Resources		Range of Victoriana resources, artefacts and web references. F11 Scaffolds. Use of TA in Jigsaw, agreeing targets and in modelling criteria.			

If all staff know what an **A8 Jigsaw** is, then no detailed explanation is necessary because the handbook or app has the full description and explanation. Visitors need only look up **A8** to see what it means. Leadership teams adopting such practice will be reassured on the rigour, quality and range of techniques in planning, and members of staff will not only use the menu to enrich their repertoire of techniques, but their precious time will now be used not for form-filling but for planning the resources that will stimulate, support and challenge the learners.

Example 3: Planning for progress 'over time'

Very few teachers deliver a topic in a single lesson that has a beginning, middle and end, so it is surprising that so many lesson-plan formats assume this to be the case. Some schools and colleges adopt a 'learning cycle' approach: learning aims → connect → new information → construct apply → review. The structure suggests that teachers plan individual lessons in this way as if each lesson is a self-contained experience. This 'cycle' will not make sense to any teacher whose learners are working over a period of time in making and doing, e.g. Art, Music, Design and Technology. For such teachers it is perfectly possible to apply the 'learning cycle' over time – anything between 4 and 12 weeks – and then the concept makes much more sense.

But it is not just teachers of practical subjects who want to plan over time. Many teachers will plan a unit of work over a number of lessons, and to create a lesson plan for each one is not only onerous but also wasteful of time, particularly if each phase includes a starter and plenary. The format below makes much more sense, particularly since many lessons are judged by leaders and inspectors on the basis of how learners are making progress 'over time'.

Lesson	Learning outcomes	Phases of lessons	Resources	Assessment	Skills
1-4	By the end of these lessons you will be able to answer the following questions: **Must:** ➤ What was it like to live in Victorian times? ➤ Why was life so different from today? **Should:** ➤ What were the main causes of poverty in Victorian slums? ➤ What does a comparison of life for the poor and wealthy show? **Could:** ➤ How did the rich people justify the differences between the poor and the wealthy? **Your final task is:** ➤ To create an original piece of writing which shows a deep understanding of one aspect of Victorian life.	1. PowerPoint showing images of Victorian times. 2. A4 groups discuss images and pose questions. 3. B5 "Learners ask the questions" objectives displayed. 4. B9 Visual map of topic produced. 5. A8 Jigsaw activity introduced. Four aspects of Victorian life. 6. A8 Jigsaw groups undertake research using scaffolds. Fact sheets on each focus created by groups. 7. Teacher and TA support. 8. ICT used (if available). 9. Back to original groups for feedback. 10. Learners select final writing task F12 from four choices. 11. G1, G2 Teacher shares criteria and models examples. 12. Learners prepare first drafts. 13. G9 Peer assessment of drafts. 14. Final draft of writing for assessment.	B5 Victorian PP and music. B9 Visual mapping. D3 Key word box. F11 Scaffolds. Wide range of books and photographs on Victorian life. Web pages listed. TA and teacher support. A4 cabaret support groups. TA support. G1 Modelled examples.	 G5 oral feedback. G5 and G6 oral feedback. G5 and G6 oral feedback. G1 modelling. Formal.	Whole class. Support groups Speaking. Small group discussion. Independent and small group research. Recording skills. Speaking skills. Paired activity. Formal writing skills

This is, in effect, a mini scheme of learning, showing the development of the topic from the introduction to the final, assessed piece of writing. It has the following features:

1. It is a plan for four lessons, not one. This cuts the workload of teachers using such a format.

2. The differentiation is the first issue to be addressed. Teachers need to start by identifying how there will be increasing challenge across the four lessons. This has been done in column two, showing planned outcomes using verbs from Bloom's and a 'must', 'should' and 'could' approach where *all* learners will attempt *all* sections (as opposed to the 'all, most, some' approach, which is unambitious and limiting).

3. The outline of activity for each lesson is set out in column three, with the codes from the handbook used and in blue for quick reference. The red line denotes the planned end of a lesson.

4. The arrow can be added with a felt pen if a visitor/observer enters the classroom – showing

exactly where the teacher is in a sequence of lessons. This is very helpful to the visitor who might only see a part of one lesson but is able to see what came before and what follows.

5. The resources in column four can include the role of the TA and how a range of resources, including ICT, are being used.

6. The assessment column identifies any AfL activity including oral feedback, sharing of assessment criteria, modelling examples, peer assessment and formal marking or tests.

7. The final column, 'skills', can include a wide range of skills activity but also other agendas such as cross-curricular or citizenship links.

8. The format works for those who want to use a 'learning cycle' approach. The main stages of connecting, engaging, introducing new information, deepening understanding and applying the learning all happen in this plan, but over four lessons, not one.

Readers who like the 'planning for progress over time' layout can download a Word version from www.robertpowelltraining.co.uk.

How to use the concepts in the book or app for reducing workload and spreading best practice.

Suggestions for a training session or workshop involving all or some staff.

1. Agree the key 'menu' headings that need to be addressed in planning outstanding lessons (e.g. 'key purpose/aims; engaging learners; differentiation, AfL etc.).

2. Identify and share the best ideas/techniques for each heading and write short descriptions of each, with examples as in the main menus of this book. Give each technique a code. This is best done within teams who teach the same age group or subject. You will end up with a wide variety within this menu. Some techniques will have applications for all staff and some will be useful only within a subject or age group.

3. Identify, share and collate additional sets of information or techniques (e.g. starters, plenaries, examination criteria or resources that might be useful to use in the

lesson planning). Store them in folders for importing later in the app.

4. Produce and publish for each team or subject a 'handbook of best practice' which captures all the best ideas/techniques coded under the main lesson-planning headings selected by the school or college.

5. The development of these handbooks has two main functions. (1) To encourage teachers to share with colleagues tried and tested classroom techniques that will eventually widen the number of lessons deemed to be outstanding. (2) To provide staff with a menu of coded techniques from which to select when planning lessons. The techniques are published in a team handbook so little detail is needed in the plan – just the heading or code. This will save teachers hours of unnecessary paperwork.

Outline of possible inset programme

(Schools that use Robert for an inset programme based on this concept will get free copies of the book – the number to be agreed based on the size of the school.)

Session 1 – Agreeing the key lesson-planning headings
(Robert Powell + SMT)

Session 2 – Build the menu

Robert Powell will introduce the menu concept and its key purpose - widening teachers' repertoires and reducing workload. Robert will share a range of techniques from the book and then teams (phase teams or departments) share techniques with each other. Teams agree which techniques to add to the menu for each main heading.

Session 3 – Developing handbooks (Teams)

Teams/departments start the production of the handbook.

Session 4 – Introduction to the app (for schools with access to iPads)

- Using the app
- Importing your own resources/menus
- Sharing lesson plans across groups of schools

If your school would like Robert Powell to lead an inset day developing such handbooks, contact him for an informal discussion on info@robertpowelltraining.co.uk

The app for iPads

The app for iPad will be launched in Spring 2016. Versions for iPhone and Android devices will follow later in the year.
The app will have the following features:

1. It will contain all the text and images from the book/pdf version.

2. Users can scroll through the menu of lesson-planning techniques selecting chapter headings at will (image 1).

3. Users can use the menu of techniques included in the app or can import their own version with their own chapter headings and menu lists - click on 'Import My Handbook' top left (image 1).

4. When users identify a technique (called a 'snippet') in the software from this menu or one that they have imported that they would like to include in the lesson they are planning, they simply scroll over the text, highlighting the words they want to move to the lesson plan, and select 'save snippet' (image 2).

   They can choose to highlight just the code, the code and title or the code, title and short description, or any other text that they want to use.

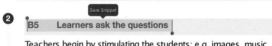

Teachers begin by stimulating the students: e.g. images, music, video, role-play, reading or a combination of these. Small groups then meet and the resulting questions are turned into lesson aims.

5. When they have selected all the techniques from the menu that they want to use users can then add other techniques e.g. starters, plenaries or curriculum objectives that have been saved elsewhere. They select 'New Snippet' and 'Add' (image 3).

Users can add a single idea or a bundle (e.g. a list of lesson starters or plenaries, or lists of syllabus criteria etc). The ones selected will be added to the snippets column as in the example 'Think, pair, share on Victorian life' starter shown at bottom left of image 4.

Users can import as many additional snippets as they choose, by typing or pasting one or more directly into the app, or by importing a special 'bundle' containing many snippets. These bundles can be created using simple text editing software on a computer such as Notepad, then imported on the iPad via an email attachment or cloud storage service such as iCloud Drive, Dropbox or Google Drive.

6. Once the list of snippets to be used is complete users import whatever lesson plan template they use onto the screen from wherever it is saved - iCloud Drive, Dropbox or Google Drive as in the right hand side of image 4.

7. They then simply drag the chosen snippets across and drop them into the appropriate section of the plan. They can select the 'Add Text' icon and add whatever additional text they require to complete the lesson plan. The text in blue in image 5 is from the snippets menu and the black text has been added by the teacher.

8. Once the lesson plan is ready users can print directly to an AirPrint printer or export as a PDF file to Email or cloud storage services such as iCloud Drive, Dropbox and Google Drive.

9. All lesson plans can be saved either for other to use or for future updating and revision (image 6).

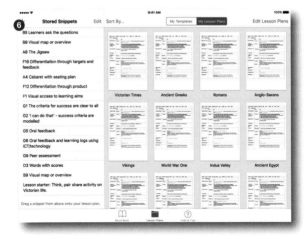